MW00917808

The Love-Based Leader

Creating Desired Results By
Overcoming Fear-Based Living

James Roswell Quinn

Jackie —
I wish for you
all of life's success,
Love "Ros"
James

"Man must evolve for all human conflict, a method,
which rejects revenge, aggression, and retaliation.

The foundation of such a method is love.
I believe that unarmed truth and unconditional love
will have the final word in reality."

Dr. Martin Luther King, Jr.

"Neither a lofty degree of intelligence nor imagination,
nor both together, go to the making of a genius.

Love, love, love, that is the soul of Genius."

Wolfgang Amadeus Mozart

ENDORSEMENTS

"James Roswell Quinn is Omni-Effective. He gets you to think, act, and change your life, and make it instantly better."
Mark Victor Hansen – Co-Creator, **Chicken Soup For The Soul**

*"**The Love-Based Leader** is a real WINNER! The great real-life stories make it a page-turner reference tool for joyful living! Quinn is bringing LOVE to a stressed-out world. TERRIFIC!"*
Ed Foreman – **U. S. Congressman** (Texas and New Mexico). The first person elected to the U.S. Congress from two different states in 100 years.

*"Learning to lead should be the focus for every successful business person. The ideas and examples in **The Love-Based Leader** provide a thoughtful approach on how to skillfully navigate an organization in the 21st century."*
Dr. Nido Qubein – **President, High Point University**
Chairman, Great Harvest Bread – President, National Speakers Association

*"Disney rarely brings in outside speakers and trainers. I am glad we decided to have Quinn run his **Love-Based Leader** workshop. Not only did everyone love the presentation, there have been noticeable changes in how people are solving problems. This was valuable."*
Joe Ranft – **Walt Disney Feature Animation, Pixar,** and **Tim Burton**
CREDITS: Cars, Finding Nemo, Toy Story, Toy Story 2, The Incredibles, Monsters Inc., The Lion King, A Bug's Life, Who Framed Roger Rabbit, Beauty & The Beast, The Little Mermaid, The Rescuers Down Under, Fantasia 2000, The Nightmare Before Christmas, Corpse Bride, and others.

*"Today's workplace poses challenging situations. Quinn's message on **Love-Based Leadership**, and recognizing the positive attributes within each of us, was inspiring and will contribute to a more balanced and constructive approach in the management of people and projects."*
Jean-Pierre St-Amand – **President, Real Property Institute of Canada**

*"Clear, powerful, memorable and inspirational. **The Love-Based Leader** delivers insightful ideas and provides the action steps to put them to work. If you want to take your life and your business to the next level, this book is your launching pad for extraordinary results. Fantastic!"*
Rich Fettke – Author of the best selling book, **Extreme Success**

"I have spoken to hundreds of Fortune 500 Companies. James Roswell Quinn is genuine, engaging, relevant and compassionate. He brings 100 years of wisdom and experience to the table. Quinn is a pro...a jaw dropper."
Brian Holloway – **Vice-President of the NFL Player's Association**
Team Captain of the New England Patriots 1985 Super Bowl Team

One Quest Publishing
P.O. Box 766
Durand, IL 61024-0766 USA

www.LoveBasedLeader.com

LoveBasedLeader.blogspot.com

Quinn@LoveBasedLeader.com

Special Pre-Release Edition

ISBN: 978-1-4515564-4-5

Foreword by Steven Sieden, Author
Buckminster Fuller's Universe, His Life and Times

Editing and Cover Design by Brandi Jasmine

Illustrations and Cover Photo by Peter Fromme-Douglas

The Love-Based Leader

Creating Desired Results By
Overcoming Fear-Based Living

James Roswell Quinn

One Quest Publishing

TABLE OF CONTENTS

FOREWORD: **Buckminster Fuller:** *The Trimtab Principle*   **7**

PREFACE: **The Leadership Evolution**   **11**

PART I – THE PROBLEM
Fear-Based Living

CHAPTER 1:   **The Four Fear-Based Reactions**   **19**

          Friendly Fred
          Feelings
          Emotions
          The Green Beret
          Fear of Failure
          Denial of Fear
          The Four Fear-Based Reactions
          The FIGHT Fear-Based Reaction
          The FLIGHT Fear-Based Reaction
          The FREEZE Fear-Based Reaction
          The FACADE Fear-Based Reaction
          EXTREME Fear-Based Reactions
          SECONDARY Fear-Based Reactions
          Position Power
          EXERCISE #1 – Your Fear-Based Reactions

CHAPTER 2:   **Fear is NOT the Problem**   **45**

          George's Story
          Resentment
          Resistance
          Revenge
          Pre-Actions and Survival Programs
          The Sand Wasp
          Non-Survival Programs
          The Three Levels of Negative Circumstances
          The Reactive Cycle
          Overcoming Fear-Based Reactions
          EXERCISE #2 – Your Non-Survival Programs

PART II – THE SOLUTION
Love-Based Leadership

CHAPTER 3: **Who Wants to WORK on a Relationship?**   **71**

Roberta Rockefeller and Me
Relating
"I Haven't Spoken To My Mother in 20 Years"
Giving Unconditionally
EXERCISE #3 - The Highest Blessing
The Man and The Wood Stove
Captain Dan and Laura
The Widow
EXERCISE #4 - Choosing To Give

CHAPTER 4: **Love-Based Leadership? In Business?**   **93**

Pro-Act
The Restaurant Manager
The Win-Win Principle
The Business World is Changing
Creating Consensus
The Distributor
Guidelines for Creating Consensus
"Well Days" at the Warehouse
EXERCISE #5 - Creating Consensus

CHAPTER 5: **Our One Quest is Peace**   **109**

The Dachau Survivor
Forgiveness
Their Daughter Was Murdered
Courage
Daniel
The Mirror Concept
LIVING Fear-Based or LEADING Love-Based
Two Flowers
The Penalty of Leadership

PART III – THE METHOD
Four E's of Excellence

CHAPTER 6:   **ETHICS - The Alternative to FACADE**   **127**

"Sarge"
ETHICS
The Problem: The FACADE Fear-Based Reaction
The Solution: Add ETHICS
The Tool: Creating Desired Results
The 7 Guidelines for Creating Desired Results
The Fired Banker
EXERCISE #6 - Creating Desired Results

CHAPTER 7:   **ENTHUSIASM - The Alternative to FREEZE**   **143**

An "Autistic" Adult
ENTHUSIASM
The Problem: The FREEZE Fear-Based Reaction
The Solution: Add ENTHUSIASM
The Tool: Planned Spontaneity
EXERCISE #7 - Plan Something Spontaneous

CHAPTER 8:   **EVALUATION – The Alternative to FLIGHT**   **157**

The Real Estate Salesman
EVALUATION
The Problem: The FLIGHT Fear-Based Reaction
The Solution: Add EVALUATION
The Tool: Centering
EXERCISE #8 - Centering

CHAPTER 9:   **EMPATHY - The Alternative to FIGHT**   **169**

EMPATHY
The Problem: The FIGHT Fear-Based Reaction
The Solution: Add EMPATHY
The New Car Dealer
The Tool: The Trust Formula
Using the Trust Formula
The Crisis Negotiator
Using the Trust Formula on Yourself
EXERCISE #9 - Creating Trust

CHAPTER 10:   **The Four Personality Styles**   **185**

The Problem With Learning Your Own Style
The Problem With Categorizing The Styles of Others
The Unique Advantage of "Four E's of Excellence"
The Love-Based Leader TARGET ZONE
Summary – Using "Four E's of Excellence" on Yourself
EXERCISE #10 – Your Love-Based Leadership Qualities
But What if "Four E's of Excellence" Does Not Work?
Summary – Using "Four E's of Excellence" on OTHERS
The Global Love-Based Leader
A Sense of Urgency
The Love-Based Leadership BOOM

James Roswell Quinn   **202**

ACKNOWLEDGEMENTS   **204**

APPENDIX: Variations of the "Four Personality Styles"   **206**

WORLDWIDE PRAISE   **227**

BIBLIOGRAPHY   **232**

A Request for Stories of *Love-Based Leadership*   **234**

Contact The Author   **235**

GET OVER YOURSELF   **237**

R. Buckminster Fuller

Businessman, statesman, inventor, futurist,

architect of the geodesic dome,

and the man who coined the term *"Spaceship Earth"*.

"Bucky" has one of the longest listings in the history of

Who's Who in America.

BUCKMINSTER FULLER
The Trimtab Principle

We find ourselves in the last stages of a great cosmic final examination. As Buckminster Fuller wrote in 1983, *"The cosmic question has been asked. Are humans worthwhile to Universe?"*

"Bucky" said our exam could be boiled down to one simple question, *"Am I choosing love or fear?"* He recognized while this choice of love over fear is actually quite logical today; it was not rational for our ancestors.

In the 1930's, Fuller was the first person to take a thorough accounting of all Earth's resources. He determined that we were continually doing *"more with less"*. Fuller surmised that our *"more with lessing"* would eventually create a world in which there was enough for everyone, and he sought to determine when that would take place.

> *"Humanity is taking its final examination. We have come to an extraordinary moment when it doesn't have to be you or me anymore. There is enough for all."*
>
> R. Buckminster Fuller

His calculations led him to predict that the shift would occur in 1976. It has now been proven that, in 1976, humankind became so efficient that we could feed everyone on Earth. That statistic also applies to all other resources including non-physical ones such as love.

There is enough of everything, but most of us continue to react from the mindset of pre-1976 when we had to fight for "our share" and to make sure that our family and friends had what they needed. We did this out of fear, which was valid prior to the 1976 transition. Now, more than ever, we need to recognize that there is enough for everyone and begin to contribute and share wholeheartedly. In other words, we need to act out of love rather than fear.

The question then becomes, how does one individual accomplish this? How can we each manifest what makes the most difference, and give our individual gifts in the most effective manner possible?

This seems like a difficult challenge until we consider all that was accomplished by the great women and men who lived in an era where there really was not enough to go around. Those brave individuals gave of themselves in ways we can only describe as heroic, even though their peers often perceived them as unstable.

These wise ancestors often used a strategy we too can employ. They looked to see where they could make the most difference with the least effort, thereby allowing them to do much more with very little. Bucky Fuller compared this behavior to that of a ship's trimtab.

"A large ship goes by, and then comes the rudder.
On the edge of the rudder is a miniature rudder called a trimtab.
Moving the trimtab builds a low pressure which turns the
rudder that steers the gigantic ship with almost no effort.
One individual can be a trimtab, making a major difference."

R. Buckminster Fuller

Bucky's tombstone reads, *"Call Me Trimtab"*

James Roswell Quinn has been a trimtab with much of his life. Rather than devoting the majority of his time to one-on-one consultation, he shares his talents and insights with groups of people. I have personally utilized many of the techniques he teaches. Quinn has a great deal to offer at this critical juncture in the evolution of humankind.

The trimtab principle is available to each of us as well. We may not be the people who stand in front of a room or write a book, but we have a responsibility to uncover our unique talents and gifts, and share them with the world in an effective manner.

Within our *"World that works for everyone"* (in Bucky's words), that has emerged since 1976, we are all vital to the process of making a global shift by becoming accountable for leading from a position of love in all aspects of our lives. We need more people who reflect this perspective of love, rather than the fear that has dominated our society since the dawn of recorded history. We need average individuals, as many leaders have described themselves, to step forward into their true calling.

James Roswell Quinn has been on the leading edge of supporting this emerging reality and the transformation that it offers to every crew member aboard Spaceship Earth. With this book, he shares a wealth of information gained from teaching hundreds of seminars and workshops.

The Love-Based Leader is a great toolbox for those seeking to make a positive difference in the world. Many have embarked on the journey toward becoming what Quinn describes as a "love-based leader". It may not always be smooth sailing, but I can assure you it is the only way our children and their children will survive and prosper.

> **"Whether humanity is to continue and comprehensively prosper on Spaceship Earth depends entirely on the integrity of the human individuals, and not on the political and economic systems."**
>
> R. Buckminster Fuller

I invite you to choose the path of love-based leadership, and become a trimtab on behalf of all humankind. Each of us can make a difference. We can contribute our gifts to others and, in the process, receive the rewards of being gifted with the talents of others.

Making the decision to be a love-based leader does not require sacrifice. The path of love is a path of joy. It promotes a sense of well being for all who choose it. Choosing love brings forth the best in each of us, and calls us to greater challenges and possibilities. Choosing love opens doorways that we did not know existed and allows for the magic called synergy to blossom in our lives and in the lives of those we touch.

In choosing to be a love-based leader, each of us helps to lay the foundation for a new civilization in which we will manifest the often-imagined "Heaven on Earth". That possibility is here now. It lies within each of us to be a trimtab, and thus make a major difference. Turn the pages of this book gently, and you will surely find clues to your personal journey.

I wish for you to live your dreams.

Steven Sieden
Author, ***Buckminster Fuller's Universe: His Life And Times***

The Evolution of Leadership

Leadership based on *Position-Power* is history.

It is time to stop fighting against what you do NOT want, and to start fighting for what you DO want.

There is a difference.

The Leadership Evolution

We are in the midst of an evolution in leadership. Throughout history, unless you were born into power or wealth, leadership was not an option. With rare exceptions, the only choice for most people was to live fear-based or die. The only choice for leaders was to lead fear-based or lose.

Today, people have a different choice. They can continue to choose to live fear-based lives, and to follow fear-based leaders. Or, they can instead choose to be love-based leaders.

The Love-Based Leader explains the fundamental concepts of this evolution. More importantly, it provides practical techniques for the development of love-based leadership as your vehicle for the creation of desired results ... personally, professionally, and globally.

For me, the quest to understand and teach the concepts and techniques of love-based leadership began in Chicago in 1975. That was the summer I was finally talked into attending my parent's LifeStream personal growth seminar. Please take a journey with me back in time.

<u>1975</u>

I am sitting in the audience, waiting for the seminar to begin. About 45 people are seated in typical seminar chairs, packed closely together, with an aisle down the center. I am sitting three rows back, on the left side of the room, facing front. There are windows to the right and rear of the room, a solid wall in front, and doors to the left. In the front of the room there is an easel stand with a large pad of paper.

Most of the people around me are chatting. I am sitting quietly by myself and wondering why I have come. My parents, who own and present this seminar, have been trying to get me here for about two years.

I am hoping this finally gets them off my back. In four days, we won't have to talk about it anymore. They will no longer be able to tell me that I am missing something special. Not only that, I will soon be able to dismiss this ridiculous concept of personal growth that they keep preaching to me. I am already looking for ways to shoot holes in the idea.

I seriously doubt that I will experience anything special, and in fact, am sitting here wondering why all of these people have paid money to my parents for this four-day, so-called, self-improvement seminar. I am sarcastically thinking, *"Did my parents withhold all of the good stuff until I paid a tuition?"* My thoughts are judgmental and resistant.

Finally, my father enters the room and begins the seminar by welcoming us all, and challenging us to be responsible for creating our own value from the weekend. *"The value won't come from what you take from this seminar,"* he tells us, *"It will come from what you are prepared to give."*

I am thinking, *"So, what is he going to be doing if we have to create the value?"* I would really rather not be here.

Then, my father looks at us and says something that changes my life. He points to the center of the audience and says,

> **"You are only as big as the smallest thing it takes to upset you."**

For some reason, that really upsets me. After all, I reason, it is not my fault if someone else is being mean or stupid. Then it occurs to me that in my lifetime, there have been many tiny little things that have upset me. All of a sudden I am thinking, *"What if my father is right? And, if he is right, if all it takes to upset me is for someone to make a stupid statement, then I must be pretty small indeed."*

I do not like having that thought, but I cannot get it out of my mind. At that moment I realize for the bulk of my life, if someone treated me badly I resented them – and if someone treated me nicely I liked them. Basically, my life had been controlled by how the people around me had been treating me. I wonder, could this explain why I am filled with so many insecurities despite all of my blessings?

I decide to discover how I can become bigger than the little things that have hurt my feelings and made me feel angry or insecure. Heck, I am tired of spending my life worrying about what everyone else is thinking anyway.

I am suddenly aware that my father is still speaking. He says, *"The bottom line is you have a choice. You can choose to live in fear and justify it, or you can choose to take responsibility for your own life and to live in love. By the end of this weekend you will know how to make that choice."* I make a conscious choice to take him up on the challenge.

Today

That was the beginning of my quest to become a love-based leader, even though my parents did not use that terminology. It has thus far led to successes far beyond my dreams.

Had I realized where this quest was going to take me, I would have certainly hesitated. My low self worth would never have allowed for me to envision speaking in nine countries, and with companies such as Walt Disney Feature Animation – much less to share the speaker's platform with world-class leaders such as Mark Victor Hansen, Jim Rohn, Les Brown, Brian Holloway, Congressman Ed Foreman, and others. No, those would have been impossible dreams for me.

If you are ready to become a love-based leader, then prepare now for the creation of successes bigger than you have ever dreamed. Not just bigger than what you have achieved, but bigger than what you have dreamed.

> It has been said that dreams are what give our lives value.
> But, it is how we live that determines if our dreams have value.

Throughout history, humans have consistently resisted change. For example, we have known for hundreds of years that there is no truth what-so-ever to the terms "sunrise" and "sunset" ... the Sun neither rises nor sets. It just appears to do so as the Earth spins on its axis. Even though this fact is common knowledge, these terms are still in general usage.

Change is now occurring so rapidly that for the first time in history, you can literally stand on a street corner and observe change taking place. Many of these changes are being resisted, to be sure. But some are being embraced.

We have seen the Internet, personal computers, cell-phones, PDAs, HD television, and other technological wonders achieve global market penetration and acceptance. This has occurred far more rapidly than anyone could have imagined just a few years ago, and the pace of change is accelerating.

Rapid changes are not just occurring in technology. In 1900, there were only 15 democracies in the world and only two in Europe. Today there are over 120 democracies in the world and only two nations in Europe are not democracies (and one of them is Vatican City).

The result of all of this change is a volatile and unpredictable world. Intimate relationships often seem to cause more frustration than fulfillment. Many families are in turmoil. A large number of corporations are floundering or failing. The United States has been involved in two wars. Fears of a global recession abound.

While people have almost always been threatened on several different fronts, the evolution of leadership is changing how people are dealing with these challenges. It is becoming increasingly unacceptable, for example, to hate the "enemy" simply because someone in power thinks we should.

Traditional "position-power" leadership has always been fear-based. By utilizing their positions of authority, husbands have controlled their wives, parents have controlled their children, bosses have controlled their employees, and governments have controlled their citizens. Position-power has been effective because most people have lived fear-based lives.

Today however, those relying on position-power are becoming increasingly frustrated because the fear-based strategies and behaviors of the past are rapidly losing effectiveness. In fact, it is becoming apparent that efforts to control others are facing more and more resistance ... personally, professionally, and globally.

Buckminster Fuller discovered that everything changed in 1976, when fear-based living shifted from being the solution to being the problem (see the "Foreword" beginning on page 7). Today, more people than ever are longing to stop living fear-based lives. *The Love-Based Leader* will show them the way.

Hard work, challenges, and threats are not new for people.
What is new is the chance for them to be leaders ...

if they choose to lead with love.

Since 1979, the concepts and techniques in *The Love-Based Leader* have been refined in over 1,500 personal and professional development seminars and keynote addresses in the USA, Canada, Mexico, Panama, Dominican Republic, Thailand, New Zealand, Bahamas, and Dubai. They have helped tens of thousands of people to overcome everything from minor irritations to unimaginable tragedies. Many of their stories are included in this book in order to assist you in solving your own personal and professional challenges.

The Love-Based Leader is your handbook for the creation of desired results with your life, not just in your life. If this stirs something in you, and you want to understand what this truly means and how to do it, then you have already begun your journey.

Regardless of your circumstances and how you feel about them, you have a choice. You can live fear-based or lead love-based. The world has enough people living fear-based. We need love-based leaders. We need you and we need you now.

Welcome to the quest,

"Ross"
James Roswell Quinn

My dream is of a joyous world where all people treat themselves,
all other people, and Earth with honor and respect.

For my children.

I love you QuinnTillions

Fear-Based Living:

The Inevitable Result of Excessive Fear-Based Reactions to Real or Perceived Threats

PART I
THE PROBLEM

Fear-Based Living

You do not need your mind to react.
An amoeba knows how to do that.

Stimulus ... Response ... Stimulus ... Response
You only need ONE cell to react.

You need your mind to be able to choose NOT to react.

CHAPTER 1

The Four Fear-Based Reactions

I was one of the lucky ones. I grew up in a family that overflowed with love. As a result I witnessed many examples of love-based leadership, long before I coined the term.

My earliest and strongest memory of the power of love-based leadership was an event that had a profound impact on both my father and me. It happened in 1966, when we were living in Thousand Oaks, California.

"Love thy neighbor as thyself."

Leviticus 19:18

Based on how most people love themselves,
our neighbors are in serious trouble.

Friendly Fred

My parents, James and Janet Quinn, were successful business owners. My father was president of the Merchant's Association, president of the Thousand Oaks Chamber of Commerce, and was on the Board of Directors of California Lutheran College. My mother was president of one of the largest Republican women's clubs in America. They also belonged to many other business, recreational, civic, and charitable organizations.

The natural consequence of their activities and friendships was a steady stream of people through our home. Add three teenagers (Nancy, Gary, and myself) plus our friends, and you can see why our house was referred to as the Quinn "Circus".

While ours was one of the most visited houses in town, I do not recall anyone ever visiting next door. Our neighbor, Fred, was the most unfriendly man I had ever known. Ironically though, he worked in public relations for a large airline company.

Every morning his garage door would open and Fred would leave for work. Every evening it would swallow him up. Fred so desired isolation he created a two-fence barrier between himself and his five backyard neighbors. Apparently, Fred did not feel just one fence was enough, because he actually built a second fence about one foot inside of the original. We jokingly nicknamed him *"Friendly Fred"*.

Friendly Fred's one love (hopefully in addition to his wife) was his beautiful dichondra lawn. Dichondra lawns are always green and never need mowing, but they do require lots of sun and water. While Southern California is blessed with lots of sun, there is not too much rain. To compensate, Friendly Fred watered his precious dichondra lawn at least once a day. The result was squishy ground ... so squishy you would leave an impression if you stepped on his lawn.

During the week, the only times we saw Friendly Fred was when he came outside to water his lawn. But on weekends, when we played football in the street or were riding our bikes on the sidewalk, Fred would come out to the curb to check for mail in his mailbox several times an hour. A dirty stare or some yelling by Friendly Fred always accompanied these little walks. He was so intimidating that if a ball or Frisbee landed in his back yard, nobody would ever knock on his door to get it back.

He was obviously consumed with protecting his property. If you have ever seen how teenagers can rebel against anyone who tries to enforce authority, then you know his fears were valid. In fact, we usually got even with him by leaving footprints and tire impressions on his beloved lawn.

Friendly Fred also resented anyone who parked in front of his house because they would leave impressions when they stepped on his lawn while going to and from their cars. It was this resentment that led to one of my greatest life lessons.

Since it was not always possible to find a parking space in front of the Quinn Circus, occasionally one of our visitors would park in front of Friendly Fred's home. Fred would immediately rush out and yell at them. We figured he must sit by his window just waiting for his chance to bolt outside and explode on any unsuspecting victim.

Friendly Fred might have been unfriendly, but he wasn't stupid. One day he bought a Rain-Bird sprinkler which sprayed water not only onto his lawn, but way out into the street. *"Now,"* he must have thought, *"nobody will park here."*

This worked like a charm, and nobody parked in front of Friendly Fred's house when he was watering. However, since he could not water his lawn all of the time, those people who parked there when the sprinkler was off would still get to experience his hostility.

One time, Friendly Fred chose to water his lawn after several cars had already parked in front of his house. When my brother and I noticed what he was doing, we started to get angry, but my father reminded us of one of his favorite sayings:

> *"When life gives you lemons, make lemonade."*

So, instead of getting angry, we decided to have a little fun at Friendly Fred's expense. Gary and I got chamois cloths, and proceeded to wash our friends" cars with Friendly Fred's water.

Friendly Fred failed to see the humor in this, and he came out and yelled at us. We simply laughed at him to rub salt in his wounds. This is basically how we lived for several years.

Then one day my parents were throwing a large party. They did not want trouble from Friendly Fred, so the invitations clearly warned everyone not to park in front of his house. Guests parked in front of other people's houses up and down the street. We were certain we would have a pleasant afternoon without having to deal with Friendly Fred.

It was a typical California summer day, hot and sunny. Most of the people were in the back yard cooking, eating and drinking. Some people were playing croquet and ping-pong while others were inside preparing food or shooting pool. Everyone was having a marvelous time.

Unfortunately, my father's good friend Bill was late for the party. Bill had just returned from a trip and had spent the morning taking delivery of his dream car, a Cadillac convertible destined to be a classic.

Bill was so excited to show off his new car that he drove straight to our party without checking his mail. He never read the invitation with the parking warning, so he pulled his car into the only remaining space; smack in front of Friendly Fred's house.

Bill joined the party and played the *"Guess what I did today"* game with us. After about an hour he told us about his new car, and we all hurried out front to see it.

To our collective horror we saw his beautiful Cadillac convertible, with the top down, being soaked by Friendly Fred's sprinkler. Apparently, just after Bill arrived, Friendly Fred had decided it was a good time to water his lawn ... and had been spraying Bill's new car with water for almost an hour.

My father literally exploded. In my 17 years, I had never seen him this angry. He was so furious he could not even talk. I honestly think you could have fried an egg on his forehead.

Suddenly, my father leapt over the little hedge separating our front yards, and ran across Friendly Fred's dichondra lawn kicking out big divots of the wet sod with each step. When he got to the sprinkler, my father kicked it so hard that instead of shooting water into Bill's Cadillac, the spray was directed into Friendly Fred's open bedroom window. He also broke his own toe.

While Friendly Fred yelled at us, we moved Bill's car into our driveway to dry it out. There was surprisingly little damage. This, however, did not cool down my father. It did not help that Friendly Fred had called the police.

Friendly Fred wanted my dad arrested for wrecking his lawn, breaking his sprinkler, and soaking his drapes. Luckily, both officers knew my father so he was not arrested. They got him to return to the party while they dealt with Friendly Fred.

By now, everyone knew about what Friendly Fred had done to Bill's car, and about how my father reacted. The party quickly lost its joyousness, and people soon departed. My father ranted all night about how he was going to get even with Friendly Fred.

The next day my father could not work because of his anger. He decided to come home early and make himself a drink. This is a man who never came home early, rarely got angry, and never got drunk. Yet there he sat, drinking in our family room with his anger increasing each minute.

About 5:30, Friendly Fred drove past our house and was swallowed into his garage. I was worried my father might go next door and start a fight.

A few minutes later, I saw Friendly Fred walking up our sidewalk. In all the years we lived next door to each other, this was the first time he had come to our home. This did not bode well.

Friendly Fred rang the bell and my dad opened the door. I was certain a fight was about to break out until I saw that Friendly Fred was crying. He looked at my dad and said, *"Jim, I just wanted to come over to apologize for yesterday."*

My father was visibly confused. *"Apologize?"*

With tears flowing, Friendly Fred continued, *"... and to thank you for the flowers."*

"Flowers?" my dad asked, really confused now.

Fred, oblivious to my dad's confusion, was holding a small card. He read from it out loud.

Dear Fred.

Isn't it silly for people to act this way?
We really do love you.

Jim & Jan

Fred was actually sobbing as he read. When he finished, Fred handed the card to my father. At that moment, my father read it to himself, *"Dear Fred. Isn't it silly for people to act this way? We really do love you."*

My father read and re-read the card, trying to figure out what was going on, until suddenly I saw him smile. As I found out later, it was then that he realized what had happened. In an attempt to solve the problems with our neighbor, my mother had sent flowers and a nice card to Friendly Fred.

But there was more. She had signed the card *"Jim & Jan"*. My mother knew my father would probably object to this love-based solution, and would have certainly refused to allow her to sign his name, so she said nothing to him about "their" little gift.

Finally, Friendly Fred said through his tears, *"Thank you Jim. I want you to know this is the first time in my life anyone has sent me flowers, and I can't tell you how much I appreciated getting them. But I really came over to thank you for something else."*

At this point, he took the card back from my father and read aloud again. *"Isn't it silly for people to act this way? We really do love you."*

Practically bawling now, Friendly Fred managed to continue: *"I want you to know, Jim, that except for my wife you are the only people in my life who have ever told me that they love me."*

With that, Friendly Fred broke down in sobs. My dad just held him in his arms, and nobody said a word for several minutes.

Finally, Fred went home, but the lesson was clear. Here we were, enjoying our "Circus" and making fun of Friendly Fred, when the only thing he really needed from us, was the one thing we had been unwilling to give to him … our love.

From that day onward, whenever anyone asked my father how to handle a difficult person, his response was always the same:

> *"Just give them love.*
>
> *Just give them love.*
>
> *Just give them love."*

<u>Feelings</u>

The previous story shows how badly things can turn when our lives are controlled by our feelings. Thankfully, it also became an example of how such negativity can be turned around with love.

Feelings are internal signals that identify both positive and negative circumstances. While good feelings can lead you to wonderful experiences, and to quality personal and business relationships, bad feelings have value as well. You jerk your hand out of a fire because you do not like the feeling of your hand burning, thus preventing great damage to your hand. This is precisely why the feeling of pain is so valuable.

Disaster can result when feelings are misinterpreted. Feelings of pleasure can lead to the trap of drug addiction. Fear of rejection has prevented many from entering into beneficial relationships.

As such, feelings are neither good nor bad, they simply exist. Examples of feelings include hunger, irritation, joy, anger, pleasure, worry, serenity, nervousness, exhilaration, anxiety, happiness, resentment, fear and longing.

> *"Einstein found two fundamental forces*
> *motivating human beings ... fear and longing."*
>
> R. Buckminster Fuller

There is a constant battle between the feelings of fear and longing. Many people long for success, but have an overwhelming fear of rejection, ridicule, success, or failure. For these people there will always be excuses instead of results, regardless of lofty goals or financial desperation.

Those whose longing for success is more important than their fears will do whatever is necessary, in spite of their fears. This creates at least the chance for success.

Many years ago, while selling advertising, I made a sale on a Friday afternoon. It was my best week ever. I was ecstatic. I knew my wife and my boss would be happy. I decided to reward myself by heading home a little early.

Then I thought, *"Why not make one more call?"* I turned the car around and saw a person whom I had been afraid would reject me. I figured, *"What have I got to lose?"* It turned out to be the single biggest sale of my career. His referrals made my next week even bigger.

Fear or longing? One will always win. When you long for success, but succumb to your fear of failure, you do not even make the attempt. But, when you overcome your fear of rejection, because you are more motivated by your longing for success, you at least make the attempt. Only then do you create the opportunity to learn from a failure, and then do it again and again until you finally succeed.

Emotions

To most people emotions are synonymous with feelings, but they are not. Feelings provide us with valuable information, while emotions are the external evidence of those feelings. Examples of emotions include laughter, tears, frowns, smiles, prejudice, kindness, cowardice, courage, shyness, arrogance, forgiveness, vengeance, resistance, hatred, and love.

In essence, emotions are how we show the world how we are feeling. Obviously, we can choose to emote our true feelings. Just as tears can be an honest expression of hurt, laughter can be an accurate demonstration of joy.

Nevertheless, emotions do not necessarily reflect or parallel our true feelings. For example, both tears and laughter can be faked. What we choose to emote is influenced by our self-worth, beliefs, desires, experiences, integrity, passions, and our current objectives.

**Fear and Resentment, as with all Feelings,
are Natural Sensations.**

**Love and Hate, as with all Emotions,
are Decisions.**

Imagine you have just witnessed your child hit by a car—not killed, but pinned under the car in great pain and terror. As you run to assist, you see an obviously drunk driver stumble out of the car. Simultaneously, you would be experiencing feelings of fear for your child, anger for the driver, and a longing for your child's survival. You would probably do one of two things:

1) Because of your feelings of fear and resentment, but in spite of or your longing for your child to be all right, you could focus on the drunk. You could chose to emote hate by attacking the drunk driver, getting hysterical, shutting-down, or even running away.

2) In spite of your feelings of fear and resentment, but because of your longing for your child to be all right, you could focus on the child. You could choose to emote love by saying things such as, *"I'm here"* or *"You're going to be OK."*

Even though you can obviously emote love even when you have feelings of fear and resentment, you would probably choose not to do so for the drunk driver (although some people may choose to forgive and then give love later). We can choose to emote love, even when we have been hurt. We can also choose to emote hate, even when we have not been hurt.

The Green Beret

Many years ago, there was a police officer in my class who literally had no fears. Officer "Smith," a former Green Beret, was a member of his department's S.W.A.T. team. He could not relate to any fear-based discussions, except from the position of being able to see how other people reacted to him because of their fears.

Officer Smith told us of his dream to become a Secret Service Agent. In fact, everything in his life had been geared to that one goal for as long as he could remember.

Unfortunately, his dream was destroyed by a single event. One night, while still in the army, he got in a bar fight because someone whistled at his date. It turned into a "Rambo" situation, with him ending up fighting the whole bar, and beating up several men. After his arrest he found out that he had lost his security clearance, and his dream was now gone. There was no chance he could ever become a Secret Service Agent.

When he finished telling us this story, I took a breath and said, *"So basically, what you are telling me is that you are a weakling. You have no power, and it's probably a good thing that you didn't become a Secret Service Agent."*

I could see his rage building as I continued, *"Let me get this straight. A guy did something you didn't like, so you had to make him pay for it. Let's see now, he spent an evening at the hospital, and you lost your dream. Who do you think paid the higher price? Who really lost?"*

> *"They hurt your feelings, your pride, and your ego for a minute.*
>
> *By reacting with rage, you hurt yourself for a lifetime."*

His jaw slackened and he just looked at me. I continued, *"You lost. You were beaten by sound waves. What a wimp."* I have never been the type of person to quit when I was ahead.

I was slowly backing up at that point because I was pretty sure I would get a reaction. But he just smiled and said, *"I understand. I think I'm getting it now. I've arrested people who've thrown their lives away because someone else made them mad. I always wondered how they could be so blind. Yet, I did exactly the same thing."*

I smiled and breathed a sigh of relief. He smiled again and said, *"You are the first person who has ever called me a name like that and walked away."* I was truly grateful he understood what I was talking about. Had he attacked me, our fight would have been a joke. While he probably knew dozens of ways of killing someone, I have never even been in a fistfight … not even once.

Fear Of Failure

Fear of failure can control your life, especially when triggered by perceived threats. These fear-based reactions must be overcome in order for you to create personal or professional excellence.

There is, for example, almost no real danger when rock climbing if you are climbing with qualified individuals in accordance with generally recognized safety standards. If you fall, your spotters and the equipment will keep you safe. Whether you feel embarrassed or inadequate, you have a choice. You can come down, continue climbing from where you fell, or try a different route.

On the other hand, for many people fear of falling creates a perception of danger that exceeds the possible good feelings they would get by successfully scaling a rock face. In such cases, otherwise capable persons give up before they start and do not give themselves a chance to experience this activity, much less excel at it.

Similarly, when a salesperson slips and falls, and fails to make a sale, there is rarely unrecoverable damage. Rejection and frustration are simply part of the process. A successful salesperson simply goes on to the next prospect, learning from the experience.

However, for many people fear of rejection creates a perception of danger that far exceeds the possible benefits of successfully making a sale. Just as with fear of falling when rock climbing, where otherwise capable persons give up before they start, they do not give themselves a chance to achieve excellence in sales.

In sales, rock climbing, or any endeavor where the perception of risk is grossly inflated, achievable objectives are not even attempted. "Playing it safe" guarantees failure. Ships in a harbor are safe, but it is not why ships were built. Avoiding the risk of failure keeps us safe, but it is not why we were born.

> **The main reason people do not have what they want?**
>
> **They are too busy trying to prevent getting what they do not want.**

Part of the problem is that "fear of rejection" and "fear of falling" are rational feelings. Rejection is painful and falling could be deadly. There is a certain amount of wisdom involved in choosing behaviors that prevent you from trying things that could end up in failure or death.

However, the cost of playing it safe can be enormous when the danger is only perceived. When you do not make a sales presentation because you hate being turned down, it is fear of rejection that has guaranteed you will not earn a commission today.

Thomas Edison did not create the light bulb by trying to prevent darkness, and you cannot create success by trying to prevent failure. You become successful by taking calculated risks, failing, learning from your mistakes and giving it another shot ... not by playing it safe.

"I've missed more than 9000 shots in my career.
I've lost almost 300 games.

Twenty-six times, I've been trusted
to take the game-winning shot and missed.

I've failed over and over and over again in my life,
and that is why I succeed. "

Michael Jordan

The answer is to develop the wisdom to identify perceived threats, and then to create the courage and determination to overcome your fears. While you will probably not succeed at everything you attempt, you will most certainly fail at everything you do not attempt.

Failure is NOT the problem.
"Fear of Failure" is the problem.

The first key to becoming a Love-Base Leader
is to overcome your fears of PERCEIVED threats.

Denial of Fear

While fears of perceived threats must be overcome, fears of real threats must be addressed and dealt with. When you deny fear, and fail to be careful when facing a genuine risk, you place yourself in danger. When you behave without considering what might go wrong, you behave as a child who spontaneously runs into the street after a ball; disaster becomes a possibility.

"If I ever lose my fear completely, I'll quit climbing."

My rock-climbing instructor in Canada

When you deny your fears, you eliminate an important source of information when making decisions. You actually place yourself in harm's way, and set yourself up for fear-based reactions when things do go wrong. Denial represents the greatest danger to "fearless" people.

The macho guy, who does not see the risk of withholding his feelings, puts his fist through a wall when his girlfriend leaves him. The arrogant teenager, who does not appreciate the consequences of shoplifting, is mortified with the thought of phoning her parents after she has been arrested. The self-centered CEO is devastated when imprisoned for "cooking the books" for personal benefit. Many people, who drive as if they are immortal, have ruined other people's lives and their own self-worth after recklessly hurting or killing someone in a car accident.

While you will probably not be able to successfully predict everything that can go wrong, you will most certainly get clobbered by the disasters you deny or ignore. Effective techniques include "Pre-Marital Counseling", "Worst-Case Scenario Planning", and "Defensive Driving".

Fear is NOT the problem.
"Denial of Fear" is the problem.

The second key to becoming a Love-Base Leader
is to address and deal with REAL threats.

The Four Fear-Based Reactions

We are all looking for happier and more fulfilled lives. Whether our desires are modest or spectacular, we often go to extreme lengths to get what we want. While we are all hoping to get lucky, we inherently know one thing ... our own actions have the primary impact on our success or failure.

Yet somehow, time after time, we self-sabotage. Sometimes we are blind to what we are doing, and of course nothing changes. At other times, even though we are fully aware we are acting in a counter-productive or even a destructive manner, we just cannot stop ourselves. Either way, it is our habitual negative behaviors that can make us each our own worst enemy.

Any such pattern, whether conscious or unconscious, is based upon fear. It could be a fear of getting something we do not want (such as rejection or physical pain), or a fear of losing something we do want (such as a relationship or a job). Either way, our own fear-based reactions are the only true barriers to our personal growth and professional development.

You may know of the "FIGHT or FLIGHT" survival theory, especially if you took a course such as Psychology 101. This concept describes the two fear-based reactions made by animals, or our ancient ancestors, who would attack or retreat when faced with physical threats.

However, these were not the only two fear-based reactions. There is a third form known as the "FREEZE". Just as a deer freezes when suddenly caught in the headlights of a car, humans have learned to protect themselves by not moving, playing dead, or hiding in a cave.

Most of us like to think of ourselves as modern rational beings. Nonetheless, even though our fear-based reactions are usually more subtle, we still tend to react to threats much as people did ages ago. Basically, we all react with FIGHT, FLIGHT, and FREEZE on a daily basis.

Couples argue and workers rant (FIGHT). People leave marriages and people quit jobs (FLIGHT). Spouses shut each other out and employees immerse themselves into busy-work (FREEZE).

Modern rational beings, however, have developed a fourth fear-based reaction that does not fit the three older categories. I call this reactive category the "FACADE" – a false front, a lie. Whether used as an attempt to hurt someone through deception or to protect oneself or another person with a white-lie, a FACADE reaction is a camouflage of the truth.

Additionally, the four fear-based reactions do not require the pre-requisite of actual danger. Simply feeling threatened is enough to trigger them. When reacting from fear, the brain believes whatever you tell it. The brain does not know the difference between what is real and what you believe to be real. Reality and perceptions are equal under the fear-based reaction process.

It is important to note that all fear-based reactions can be appropriate responses to actual threatening circumstances. Unfortunately, they can also become habits that may evolve into automatic patterns, even when there is no real threat. Since habits by definition are "non-think" behaviors, in times of stress they can cause you do something you will come to regret ... often leaving you with considerable personal and professional consequences.

Instead of leaving your life to chance, the key to success is to identify and overcome your fear-based reactions to negative circumstances. Think of this book as your "tool kit" in this quest for self-control.

It is by becoming aware of your obvious fear-based reactions that it will become easier for you to identify your more subtle ones. As you read the following descriptions, try to determine your most common reactive patterns.

All of us have two things in common.

**1) We each have a tendency towards two
of the four Fear-Based Reactions.**

2) We each will occasionally demonstrate the other two.

The FIGHT Fear-Based Reaction

When demonstrating a FIGHT fear-based reaction you give ultimatums, get sarcastic, become vengeful, yell, or even attack someone physically. Whether you are actively seeking to fix something, finish something, or punish someone…you say exactly what you mean. You are, or can appear to be, unconcerned about the needs and feelings of others.

You will hear yourself asking "What?" types of questions:
"What's your problem?" … "What are you going to do about it?"

When Negatively Consumed With RESULTS,
Your Primary Characteristic Tends to Be JUDGMENTAL.

"I don't get mad, I get even."
"If you want something done right, you've got to do it yourself."
"The end justifies the means."

Other FIGHT Characteristics:

Aggressive   Manipulative   Arrogant   Sarcastic   Critical
Demanding   Intimidating   Insensitive   Offensive   Argumentative

---

The Extreme FIGHT Fear-Based Reaction: PARANOID

Ask yourself,
"Do I tend to be blunt with criticism and judgment?"

The FLIGHT Fear-Based Reaction

When demonstrating a FLIGHT fear-based reaction you panic, make excuses, rush, motor-mouth, or interrupt others. Whether you are trying to find something for someone, make it to an appointment, or get away from someone … you say the first thing that comes to your mind. You are, or can appear to be, not listening to anyone else.

You will hear yourself asking "Who?" or "When?" types of questions:
"Who do you think you are?"… "Who is going to be there?"
"When is the appointment?"… "When will you finally start listening to me?"

When Negatively Consumed With RELATIONSHIPS,
Your Primary Characteristic Tends to Be FRANTIC.

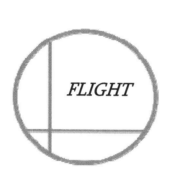 

"I don't have to take this, I'm out of here."
"Don't worry about it. I'll take care of it later."
"I've got too much to do and not enough time to do it."

Other FLIGHT Characteristics:

Distracted   Overwhelming   Harried   Panicked   Hyperactive
Impulsive   Hurried   Excitable   Pushy   Scattered

The Extreme FLIGHT Fear-Based Reaction: HISTRIONIC (Frenzied)

Ask yourself,
"Do I easily become panicked?"

33

The FREEZE Fear-Based Reaction

When demonstrating the FREEZE fear-based reaction you become analyzing, isolated, and generally avoid others. Whether you are trying to get something right, figure something out, or avoid a relationship … you do not even speak until you have had the time to collect your thoughts. You are, or can appear to be, disconnected from others.

You will hear yourself internally asking "How" types of questions:
"How can you say that to me?"
"How can I do all of this?"

When Negatively Consumed With TASKS,
Your Primary Characteristic Tends to Be OVERWHELMED.

"I don't want to talk about it."
"In the time it takes to explain, I can do it myself."
"If you can't say something nice, don't say anything at all."

Other FREEZE Characteristics:

Anxious   Inward   Picky   Withdrawn   Apprehensive
Serious   Shameful   Tense   Isolated   Shut-Down

The Extreme FREEZE Fear-Based Reaction: AVOIDANT

Ask yourself,
"Do I generally avoid confrontation?"

The FACADE Fear-Based Reaction

When demonstrating a FACADE fear-based reaction you strive to make things look better than they really are. Whether you are trying to protect yourself or someone else, you say what you think others can handle, or what you feel they want to hear. You are, or can appear to be, lacking integrity or lying.

You will ask yourself or others "Why?" types of questions:
"Why me?" … "Why can't we just get along?"
"Nothing's wrong, why do you ask?"

When Negatively Consumed With FEELINGS & EMOTIONS,
Your Primary Characteristic Tends to Be WORRIED.

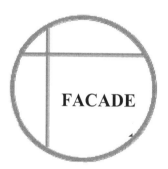 

I say one thing to your face, but I'm thinking something else.
Out loud, *"I'm fine. I'm just fine."* Inside, *"I'm hurt and angry."*
Out loud, *"I'll buy your product."* Inside, *"I'll cancel tomorrow."*

Other FACADE Characteristics:

Intimidated   Defensive   Phony   Subordinate   Guarded
Guilty   Insecure   Inferior   Fragile   Needy

The Extreme FACADE Fear-Based Reaction: DEPENDENT

Ask yourself,
"Do I usually feel responsible for other's feelings?"

EXTREME Fear-Based Reactions

When you develop habitual fear-based reactive patterns, over time you risk exaggerating them. These "Extreme" fear-based reactions can actually resemble psychological disorders.* Is it ever in your best interest to be viewed as such?

FIGHT becomes PARANOID when everything is a threat.

FLIGHT becomes HISTRIONIC when there is always a crisis.

FREEZE becomes AVOIDANT when the solution is to have no relationships.

FACADE become DEPENDENT when you always think, *"Don't rock the boat."*

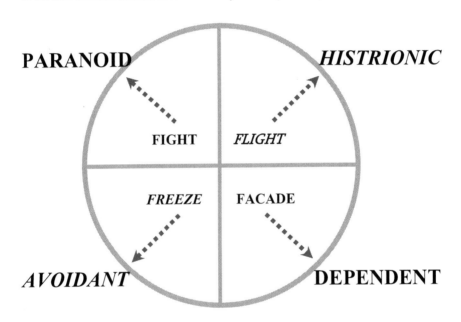

*Abnormal Psychology, Seligman, Walker & Rosenhan, 2000

The FIGHT Reaction can become PARANOID behavior:

When the FIGHT reaction becomes a habit, we not only attack real threats, we eventually begin to attack perceived threats as well. As we become more sensitive to perceived threats, more circumstances trigger this reaction, and paranoia eventually sets in. Woody Allen once said, *"It isn't paranoia if they really are out to get you."* However, if you have ever spent any time with a paranoid person, you know how any little thing can make them lose control.

The FLIGHT Reaction can become HISTRIONIC behavior:

When we were kids, my grandmother used to tell us, *"Quit running around like chickens with your heads cut off."* Some people leave jobs or relationships at the first sign of a challenge. Others become chatterboxes and push others away with fidgety, hyperactive behavior. Either way, the results are the same. People who run away from problems are usually running toward new ones. The only thing that changes is how much easier it becomes to trigger the next histrionic episode.

The FREEZE Reaction can become AVOIDANT behavior:

The FREEZE reaction can easily grow into a pattern of avoidance, mostly because of the temporary sense of peace it can bring. However, the long-term costs of shutting down overshadow any short-term gains. Corporations need leaders who are quickly able to address challenging situations, and predict problems rather than avoiding them. All relationships require active involvement. Anyone who ignores small problems only guarantees larger problems later.

The FAÇADE Reaction can become DEPENDENT behavior:

FACADE reactions can develop into outright lies when a person spends considerable time worrying about the feelings and reactions of others. These often take the form of "little" white lies, but they are lies nonetheless. Increasingly, as this behavior becomes one of dependence, self-worth slips away. The only way this person can feel good is when someone else makes them feel good. Unfortunately, when another person is in charge of your happiness, they are also in charge of your unhappiness. Or, as my father used to say, *"You give them the whole ball of wax."*

Ask yourself (and be honest),

"Which Extreme Fear-Based Reactions have I ever demonstrated?"

SECONDARY Fear-Based Reactions

While everyone periodically exhibits all four of the fear-based reactions, as creatures of habit, we all tend to use one fear-based reaction more often than the rest. Additionally, we each have one or two "Secondary" fear-based reactions that occur almost as often.

A secondary fear-based reaction usually occurs immediately after the primary fear-based reaction. For example, some people verbally or physically abuse their spouse or lover in a fit of rage (FIGHT), then later apologize and promise, *"It will never happen again"* (FACADE). In this abuse cycle, the FACADE follows the FIGHT as a secondary fear-based reaction.

My own reaction cycle is just the opposite. FACADE is my primary fear-based reaction. When threatened, I tend to worry about the other person's feelings more than my own. My behavior is affected accordingly, as I do not want to upset anyone. However, if I am feeling attacked or unappreciated, I can easily move into FIGHT (generally in the form of anger or sarcasm) as my secondary fear-based reaction.

Another common scenario is FACADE followed by FLIGHT. People will say, *"Everything is fine,"* when everything is really not fine, and then run away as quickly as possible. This is the pattern used when a spouse or lover says, *"I love you"*, and then leaves the relationship shortly thereafter. This is also the pattern used when a customer places an order when face-to-face with the salesperson, but calls to cancel the next day.

PRIMARY	SECONDARY
FIGHT	FLIGHT, FREEZE, or FACADE
FLIGHT	FIGHT, FREEZE, or FACADE
FREEZE	FIGHT, FLIGHT, or FACADE
FACADE	FIGHT, FLIGHT, or FREEZE

Many people can have difficulty identifying their primary fear-based reaction, especially when they have a secondary fear-based reaction that occurs quite frequently. Do not worry if you have trouble distinguishing them.

The important thing is to identify the fear-based reaction you are making, while you are making it. Only then, regardless of whether it is a primary or secondary reaction, can you make a conscious decision to overcome it.

SECONDARY Fear-Based Reactions

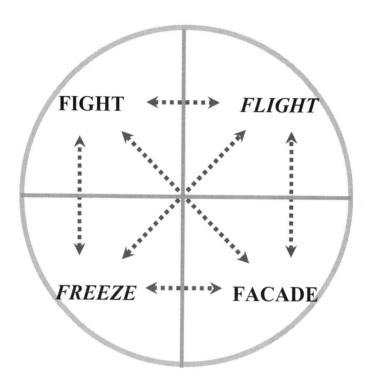

**Your Secondary Fear-Based Reactions may be
INDEPENDENT of your Primary Fear-Based Reaction.**

<u>For Example:</u>

You could have a **Primary Fear-Based Reaction of FREEZE**,

with a Secondary Fear-Based Reaction
of **FACADE at work,**

and another Secondary Fear-Based Reaction
of **FIGHT at home.**

Position Power

Everyone is on a quest for success. The desire may be for love, financial gain, improved health, increased leadership, advancement within an organization, or better relationships. Whatever the quest, assistance and inspiration can be acquired from a multitude of sources.

Self-Help books, eBooks, DVDs, CDs, blogs, and magazine articles abound. One can attend personal growth seminars, sales management workshops, parenting classes, encounter groups, Alcoholics Anonymous, Overeaters Anonymous, health-clubs, and marriage encounters (information about my high-impact LifeStream and LifeResults professional and personal growth workshops and seminars can be found at www.LoveBasedLeader.com). Guidance is available from churches, school teachers, counselors, therapists, psychologists, psychiatrists, radio call-in shows, suicide hot-lines, psychics, astrologers, business consultants, life coaches, keynote speakers, gurus, Dear Abby, Dr. Phil McGraw, and your parents.

Nevertheless, whether your motivation is selfless or selfish, for love or for profit, virtually everything available to you requires the development of your ability to get others to change something. You are told that if you act in a certain manner people will change how they treat you. Ask the right questions and a prospect will change their attitude and buy your product, or join your organization. Treat your resistant partner correctly and they will give you love. It may not always seem like you are trying to control others, but if the objective is to change the behaviors of others—it is control nonetheless.

Control has always been successful in at least some situations and with certain people. But, its effectiveness is diminishing rapidly. As such, the vast majority of resources miss the point:

> **All attempts to control others are focused on the wrong person.**
>
> ***Leadership Effectiveness* is an Art ... *The Art of Self-Control.***

- For some people, self-control means toughness: ***"I don't get mad, I get even."*** (FIGHT)

- For others, it is all about leaving a way out, just in case something goes wrong: ***"I don't have to take this, I'm out of here."*** (FLIGHT)

- For many, self-control is the ability to refrain from hurting others, even when they are hurt or angry: ***"If you can't say something nice, don't say anything at all."*** (FREEZE)

- And yet for others, self-control means to never rock-the-boat. ***"Tell people only what they want to hear,"*** or ***"Tell people only what you think they can handle."*** (FACADE)

Statements such as these may seem like self-control to most people. But in reality, they are all attempts to control others. People who are justifying these behaviors are either trying to get someone else to do something (i.e. buying your product), or trying to prevent them from doing something (i.e. leaving an intimate relationship).

Unfortunately, whether striving to be helpful or self-serving, the only way to ensure success with these tactics is to establish some kind of position-power over others. As such, employers, managers, salespeople, elected officials, police officers, parents, spouses, and life-partners ultimately strive to get what they want by establishing or enforcing the power of their position.

Position-Power is nothing more than a Fear-Based justification to control others. This can be a Fear OF others, *"You might hurt me,"* or it can be a Fear FOR others: *"You might hurt yourself."*

Position-power may be expressed blatantly with orders, threats, demands, hysterics, and ultimatums. However, this manipulation can also be demonstrated in more subtle ways, such as by shutting down, backing away, and by outright lies. Nevertheless, whenever you attempt to control someone else, you have just become the problem.

Most people are their own worst enemies. To create desired results as a love-based leader, you need to overcome fear-based impulses to exert position-power. Or, as I say in my seminars, keynotes, and CDs: *"Get Over Yourself."*

Regardless of the intent, anyone using position-power to control others is facing increasing resistance. Modern persons in democratic societies do not function under a strict and inflexible hierarchy as our ancestors once did. In fact, we resist and resent those who attempt to control us, even when we are told, *"This is for your own good."* Just ask any teenager.

Controlled children may not rebel but, at best, they will have a limited relationship with their parents when they become adults. A spouse can control their partner or children but, in so doing, will typically destroy their love, respect, and affection. Dishonest or incongruent salespeople may initially make money, but sales from repeat business and referrals are rare. Dictatorships may seem to be effective, but history teaches us that assassinations and revolutions are the inevitable outcomes.

In the short term, position-power can give intimate, family, and business relationships the illusion of effectiveness. However, people with high levels of self-worth are finding such fear-based environments increasingly unacceptable. They have found, and will continue to find, better places to live and work.

Those who remain usually see the levels of fear increase in direct proportion to the deterioration of the family or business. The cycle will continue until excellence and passion are stifled. Personal and professional relationships which operate within this paradigm cannot flourish. Resentment and resistance ultimately lead to sabotage, diminished results, and even destruction. The good news is there is an alternative to position-power.

The old fear-based patterns are changing. People are beginning to realize they are merely creating new problems whenever they justify fear-based reactions to challenging or threatening circumstances.

Position-power is losing ground to effective, innovative and forward thinking love-based leaders who are striving to create loving relationships, joyful families, business success, or effective government.

> **It is becoming increasingly apparent that positive results**
> **will come through leaders ... not from them.**

First, you must establish self-control. Only then does it become appropriate to try and help others identify and change their negative, non-productive, and destructive behaviors. Until that time, such attempts will likely be unsuccessful or short-lived.

To be effective, a leader must become aware of his or her fear-based reactions and make necessary decisions to overcome them. Love-based leadership is a skill that can be sharpened and made more effective by increasing the capacity to think, reason, and make conscious choices. *The Love-Based Leader* teaches you how to overcome stress and create positive results, first by becoming aware of your own negative position-power fear-based reactions and then by changing them.

Instead of focusing on what others are doing wrong, take responsibility for changing yourself. Your leadership will be greatly enhanced.

The truth is, the reactions of others are merely measurements of your own effectiveness, or lack thereof. When you become aware of your own negative position-power fear-based reactions, it becomes easier for you to see how you are attempting to control others with actual or implied position-power, and therefore easier to make alternative choices.

What are your primary fear-based reactions? What are your secondary fear-based reactions? Sometimes it helps to think about recent situations where you felt some regret about your behaviors. Consider criticisms you have received. It is important to be honest here. Watch out for "denial".

While it is easy to categorize the reactions of other people, courage is needed for an honest self-evaluation. The following exercise will help you to get clear on your own primary and secondary fear-based reactions. Review the following four lists and circle everything you tend to demonstrate when things go wrong.

Everyone demonstrates all of these qualities from time to time, but your results should at least give you a good idea which one or two fear-based reactions you tend to display most often. Your primary and secondary fear-based reactions will be the two with the highest numbers. Once you learn how to overcome your two most obvious fear-based reactions, it will become easier to deal with the more subtle ones.

EXERCISE #1 - Your Fear-Based Reactions
Circle Your Most Frequent Negative Reactions

List A	List B	List C	List D
Aggressive	Distracted	✓ Anxious	✓ Defensive
✓ Argumentative	Excitable	✓ Apprehensive	✓ Fragile
Arrogant	Frantic	✓ Inward	✓ Guarded
Critical	Harried	Isolated	✓ Guilt
Demanding	Hurried	✓ Overwhelmed	✓ Inferior
Intimidating	Hyperactive	Picky	✓ Insecure
Insensitive	Impulsive	Serious	Intimidated
Judgmental	Overwhelming	Shameful	✓ Needy
Manipulative	Panicked	✓ Shut-Down	Phony
Offensive	Pushy	✓ Tense	✓ Subordinate
Sarcastic	Scattered	✓ Withdrawn	✓ Worried

Total the number of circled items in each column:

7   9

FIGHT   **FLIGHT**   **FREEZE**   **FACADE**

Your PRIMARY Fear-Based Reaction (the highest number)   *Facade*

Your SECONDARY Fear-Based Reaction (the 2nd highest number)   *Freeze*

Helpful Hints:

If you will not do this exercise,
your PRIMARY Fear-Based Reaction is probably FIGHT.

If you feel you exhibit all four reactions equally,
your PRIMARY Fear-Based Reaction is probably FLIGHT.

If you are stuck and cannot decide,
your PRIMARY Fear-Based Reaction is probably FREEZE.

If you worry about getting it right,
your PRIMARY Fear-Based Reaction is probably FACADE.

The Four Fear-Based Reactions

"**When you react to your fear,
you do everything exactly wrong.**"

My ski instructor in New Zealand

CHAPTER 2

Fear is NOT the Problem

I t is easy to be love-based—energized, caring, confident, and peaceful—when everything is fine. The trick is to be able to do so when faced with unwanted circumstances.

Unexpected challenges such as unemployment, harassment, crime, abuse, divorce, illness, accidents, injury, and death are unpleasant events to be sure. However, they are not the problem. The problem occurs when such events trigger your negative fear-based reactions.

Having Fear is NOT the Problem.

Getting Rid of Fear is NOT the Solution

Fear-based reactions may take the form of white lies, manipulation, panic, nasty facial expressions, sarcasm, insincere agreements, shutting down, phony smiles, nervous laughter, jokes, or yelling. They can also be as severe as avoiding clients, refusing to phone prospects, quitting jobs, firing employees, dropping out of school, running away from home, divorce, child abuse, drunk driving, drug abuse, suicide, murder, or war.

It is important to remember that fear itself is not the problem. We all feel fear. It is a natural response to a threatening situation. It is our negative reactions to fears that create our problems. These reactions occur when we are either overwhelmed by fears of perceived threats, or as a direct result of having been in denial of our fears of real threats. Either way, the answer is always the same ... love-based leaders overcome automatic, non-think, fear-based reactions.

George's Story

The names are fictitious, but the following story is true. About 1950, George's friend Bob started a company in Thousand Oaks, California. Bob became the president of the new company, and the majority stockholder. David, the vice-president, was the financial backer and held most of the remaining shares.

George was hired as the plant manager and was given a small share in the company. Bob promised George, *"Don't worry. You will be taken care of when the business succeeds."*

Even though his salary was less, and he had far fewer shares than the other partners, for all intents and purposes, George considered it to be his company. For the next 25 years he worked days, evenings, weekends, and even on holidays when needed.

Because of the teamwork, friendship, and abilities of the three partners, the company became a profitable business employing over 300 people. This was one of those companies from which people never quit, and where there was rarely a firing. It was a big event whenever there was a marriage, birth, or retirement. It was more like a family than a business.

Then one day, David announced his retirement. A little later, George got a note from the boss:

George,

I need to meet with you at 9:00 tomorrow morning. We have something very important to discuss.

Bob

As most people would do, George immediately began thinking something like, *"Twenty-five years and finally I will get the promotion I deserve."* He was certain that he would get a raise and a larger share of the company.

Of course, George could not wait to tell his wife the good news. He got home early to tell her, and she almost burst into tears with joy. She exclaimed, *"We've waited so long for this!"*

George's wife then told him that the beautiful home they had dreamed of owning was up for sale. This house was on a hillside with a beautiful swimming pool and a breathtaking view of the entire Conejo Valley. With a larger salary, plus the equity in their home, they were certain they would qualify for a loan. All evening their excitement continued to grow.

George got very little sleep that night, and in the morning his wife fixed him a wonderful breakfast. As he left for work his wife called out, *"Don't forget to call."* George was deeply in love with his wife, and hugely appreciative of her years of quiet support. He knew that he could never have achieved this without her.

George got to his office full of anticipation, and got to the boss's office early. George was waiting as the boss entered and said. *"Good morning, George, come on in,"* and he told his secretary to hold all calls.

"As you know," he began, *"David is retiring and we need to replace him. George, I want you to be the first to know that I'm bringing my cousin Horace in from Toronto to be the new vice-president. I need for you to teach him the business."*

Remember, this is a true story.

How would you feel if this were happening to you?

George immediately exploded with anger and demanded an explanation. The boss bluntly replied, *"George, I need to hire Horace in this position and you're the one person I can count on to make sure he is properly trained. I need you to do this for me. I can't get into it now. But, don't worry; I'll take care of you."* Then, without further explanation, the boss left the building.

George left the boss's office dazed, but filled with resentment. He was resenting the boss, Horace, David and most especially, himself.

Negative thoughts were racing through George's head. *"Twenty-five years. He promised me. How can he treat me like this?"* The resentment kept building. *"I made this company for him! He's gotten rich off of me. He's taken vacations I could never afford. This is the thanks I get? I trusted him."*

At this point, George moved from resentment to resistance. He resisted calling his wife. He resisted working. He just sat at his desk, suffering ... until he finally headed for a bar. Then, about 2:00AM, he went home.

George's wife had been waiting all day for the phone call about the promotion. Instead, he came home late, drunk, and angry. Things got much worse when he told her the "good news" about Horace.

"How can you let them treat you like this?" She shouted. She resented Bob, Horace, and especially George. She even resented herself for supporting George for so many years. She stormed off to the bedroom. George slept on the couch, and fixed himself cold cereal for breakfast.

The next morning, George arrived late for work. His resistance was increasing with thoughts such as, *"After all, I've worked weekends, nights, and even holidays for this company. I've earned a late morning, and then some."*

At the office, Bob introduced George to Horace, and asked him to take the new vice-president around the plant to meet everyone. George reluctantly agreed.

47

"This is Horace, our new vice-president," he told them. *"He is going to show us how to make our company work."* George winked and gave smirks to these people who were his close friends. His resentment and resistance spread, and many people became angry and resentful because George was not promoted.

Upon returning to the office, George was introduced to Horace's wife. She and the boss's wife had been house-hunting all morning. *"Horace, you'll never believe the house we found,"* she gushes. *"It's a beautiful home up in the hills, with a swimming pool and a breathtaking view."*

"My God," George thought. *"They're buying our dream house. If my wife finds out about this ..."* He could not even finish this thought because of his fear of her reactions. His resentment was growing.

Horace's wife continued, *"Bob has agreed to help us with the down payment. Let's go see it and make an offer right now!"* That was about all George could stand. He began thinking of how to get his revenge.

George took money from petty cash and headed for the racetrack. *"I've earned it,"* he justified. *"Besides, I'll pay it back. They owe me a chance to win a little money."* Of course, he lost it all.

His resistance was intensifying. George spent almost no energy training Horace, but a great deal of time in the plant with his friends, venting his anger at the boss and at Horace. Otherwise, he continued losing money at the track almost every day.

Suddenly, his thefts were discovered shortly after the president called for a surprise audit. While he did not call the police, Bob felt he had no choice but to fire George from the only job he ever loved.

Unfortunately, George's tribulations were not over. Not long after he was fired, his wife left him. His children were so angry about how badly he had hurt their mother that they never spoke to him again. George lost his job, his marriage, and his family. Eventually, he went bankrupt, become an alcoholic, and died a lonely and bitter shell of a man.

This is a sad story. Nevertheless, it is not why it is being shared here.

You see, there is one thing George never knew. Bob could not bring himself to tell George or anyone else that he had just found out he was dying of cancer. He was consumed with two things, and two things only ... the survival of his company and the financial needs of his wife.

It turns out that Bob feared that if news of his condition reached his customers, they might lose confidence and shift to a different supplier. Bob also thought that if the company were sold, his loyal employees might lose their jobs. He decided to hide the truth (the Freeze and Facade reactions), and devised a scheme.

First, Bob bought back David's shares in the company and persuaded him to retire. Next, he arranged for Horace to move to Thousand Oaks and become the new vice-president. Bob wanted Horace to learn the business from George because, in return for his many years of loyal service and friendship, he was going to give the company to George.

Bob knew that George would run the company properly and that the employees would gladly work for him. The only condition was that George would share the profits with Bob's wife for as long as she lived. Bob felt he could trust George, and that he really did deserve to be the president and owner.

However, because of his justified fear-based reactions due to his resentments, George lost it all. Not long after George was fired, Bob died. Horace was incapable of running the company, and since he had no support from the employees, it soon went out of business.

The shares Bob was going to give to George became worthless. Bob's wife was forced to live with her children. Three hundred dedicated employees lost their jobs, with incalculable effects on their family's lives. After everything was said and done, George's behavior hurt his wife, his family, the boss's wife, and his co-workers and their families.

Who loses when you justify Fear-Based Reactions

because of Resentment?

EVERYONE

The question before the house is, "What alternatives did George have?" Actually, he had several.

1. George could have quit and formed his own company. He had the personal resources and the banking connections to do this. Additionally, most of the good employees and most of the customers would have readily followed him. Could George have overcome his RESENTMENT to create his own company?

2. He could have quit and gotten a better job with a company that appreciated his value, and there were several who would have taken him in a heartbeat. Again, most of the employees and customers would have followed him. Could George have overcome his RESENTMENT to get a better job?

3. George could have re-committed himself to the existing company and trained the new man as requested, thus further solidifying his position with his boss (which is exactly what would have happened in this case). Could George have overcome his RESENTMENT to improve this company? To be sure, this was unlikely. But was it possible?

But instead of these alternatives, and because of his resentment, George chose a path that led to the destruction of virtually everything he cared about. This is the path of the "Three Stages of Fear-Based Reacting". Once begun, it is very hard to get off of this path.

RESENTMENT
The First Stage of Fear-Based Reacting

RESENTMENT is the first stage of fear-based reacting. Resentment by itself is not the problem, it is a natural feeling. Just as you feel joy when someone pleases you, you feel resentment when someone hurts you. You can even resent yourself. But it is what you do because of the feelings of resentment, or in spite of them, that determines if you are leading from love or reacting from fear.

You have almost certainly resented the people who have hurt you, your family, your friends, your company, your faith, or your country. You have also resented people who controlled you, or who even attempted to control you, even when they were doing it, *"for YOUR own good."*

You may also have resented others when you were unable to control them, even when you believed what you were doing was *"for THEIR own good,"* or for the good of your family, or your company. Regardless of your initial justifications for resentment, if you do not overcome your resentments, your fear-based reactions will escalate.

All acts of aggression and retaliation have one thing at their base:

RESENTMENT

Yes, we resent people we hate. However, as any parent who has resented a child who did not listen to them knows, we can also resent people we love. For this reason, people are often perplexed by their own resentment. However, as with all feelings, resentment has a purpose. You do not enjoy the feelings of resentment, but they do have value. They inform you that you have been hurt.

Imagine your hand is burning in a fire. Pain tells you to remove your hand before it is permanently damaged. Nobody enjoys the sensation of pain when being burned, but there is value in the pain because it makes you respond quickly and thus avoid greater injury.

If you were to treat your burning hand the same way many people typically handle resentment in an argument, instead of removing your hand you would probably say something such as, *"The fire should change. Why should I move my hand? The fire should not be treating me this way. After all, I've given it the best years of my life!"* But the damage would still continue.

Likewise, when you justify your fear-based reactions because of resentment, the damage to yourself and others also continues. Additionally, because fear-based reactions tend to escalate the scale of damage, solutions become progressively more difficult to implement at each successive stage.

RESISTANCE
The Second Stage of Fear-Based Reacting

After Resentment, the second stage of fear-based reacting is RESISTANCE. Do not confuse resistance with caution. In many situations, caution is necessary for survival.

Resistance, on the other hand, is a signal you are no longer in control of yourself or your destiny, and that the choices you are making are ultimately not in your best interest. Resistance is self-destructive and does nothing to create self-worth, quality relationships, or business success.

Resistance can be expressed in many ways. People who feel unappreciated resist giving 100% in a job. Shy people resist sharing, even if they hate themselves for not speaking up. Angry people resist being patient and giving love, despite the fact the people they care about are being pushed away. Battered women resist leaving abusive husbands, while living in terror. Frightened people resist new relationships, even when they loathe being alone.

What is the normal reaction to change?

RESISTANCE

(Even if what you are doing is not working)

It is obvious that resistance to removing your hand, when you feel pain in a fire, would be destructive to your hand. What is not so obvious is that resistance to changing your behavior, when you feel resentment in an argument, is just as destructive to yourself and your relationships. Pain and resentment are feelings intended to inform you of danger. Resistance to these signals can be disastrous.

Sometimes, you justify your resistance to expressing hurt or anger because you do not wish to upset people whom you care about, or whom you fear. *"After all,"* you may rationalize, *"it was really not a big deal,"* and you repress your negative feelings. Eventually these feelings will become stronger than your resistance to expressing them.

Additionally, most people have resisted themselves from time to time. Have you ever resisted sharing your thoughts and feelings, perhaps out of a fear of being rejected, used, laughed at, or criticized?

Yes, it can be difficult to implement love-based solutions at the Resistance Stage. Nevertheless, whether the resistance is to yourself or someone else, it is far easier here than attempting to do so at the third stage of fear-based reacting.

REVENGE
The Third Stage of Fear-Based Reacting

After Resentment comes Resistance. Unless a conscious choice is made at that point, REVENGE (the third stage of fear-based reacting) becomes inevitable.

Revenge comes with a built in irony. While it targets others in an attempt to get-back-at, get-even-with, or get-away-from them, revenge carries elements of self-sabotage, or even self-destruction, as we develop emotional reactions, and programs of hatred. In fact, revenge by us can easily become more damaging to us than what has been done to us.

As with resistance, revenge can take many different forms. Theft, sabotage, divorce, abuse, ridicule, destruction of property, violence, and murder are but a few examples. People have even been known to destroy themselves with drugs and suicide, in order to hurt someone else.

> *"When you hurt someone else, you hurt yourself a lot worse."*
>
> **Your Grandmother**

Vengeance targets people you hate, such as those who have abused you or who have abused a loved one, a friend who let you down, the "other" man or woman, a thief, your ex-spouse, or an employer. When you blame your negative behaviors on another person, destruction will ultimately result. Your reaction becomes the other person's negative circumstance, which increases the chances for them to react (again).

George, for example, rationalized his thefts from petty cash to fund his trips to the race-track. He wanted to get even with his lifetime friend (his boss) for passing him over for the big promotion.

Revenge can also be directed at people whom you care about. You might spank a child for embarrassing you. You may gossip about a co-worker friend who got "your" promotion. You can even take revenge on yourself if you are upset at something you did, or did not do. Revenge always feels justified.

When you react often enough, eventually your negative behaviors will not even need a trigger to occur. Ultimately, revenge is not a behavior. It is a self-image.

Pre-Actions and Survival Programs

People tend to have a fear-based reaction when threatened with a negative situation. If there is any perceived benefit associated with that fear-based reaction, the behavior is likely to be repeated when faced with the same or similar circumstance.

A fear-based reaction, when repeated enough, eventually occurs prior to the negative circumstance, *"Just in case."* This behavior is no longer a reaction ... it is now a "Pre-Action".

Pre-Actions

Conscious Fear-Based behaviors, which occur BEFORE negative circumstances (real or perceived) NOT as a result of them.

For example, a small boy cries when he falls and hurts himself. This is a natural response to pain. However, he often learns the lesson that it is unacceptable for boys to show their feelings. He may hear, *"Don't be such a baby," "Have a stiff upper-lip," "Be a man,"* or the classic, *"If you don't stop crying, I'll give you something to cry about."* He might even get a spanking. His father may be cruel and insensitive, or he could be concerned that his son may get picked on for being a crybaby.

Regardless of his father's intentions, because he is experiencing consequences for crying, eventually the child may conclude, *"Crying only makes things worse."* Then one day he hurts himself and starts to cry, but is able to hold back his tears ... on purpose.

This choice to refrain from crying around his father is a conscious pre-action, with a clear perceived value ... he is either praised or ignored by Daddy. To the little boy, either response is far superior to spankings, threats, or ridicule. With this validation, his pre-action of withholding tears is likely to be repeated until it becomes an unconscious habit ... a "Survival Program".

Survival Programs

Pre-Actions that are repeated until they occur unconsciously.

Unfortunately, survival programs, because they are unconscious, can easily render what was originally an effective pre-action to become non-productive, negative, or even self-destructive. It does not take much to change survival programs into self-sabotaging "Non-Survival Programs".

The Sand Wasp

Once upon a time, some scientists were studying sand wasps. While observing their eating habits, they discovered a strange habit indigenous to the species.

Every morning the sand wasps scoured the desert for food. Usually they found a dead fly or some other bug. However, instead of eating the meal out in the open, the sand wasps would carry the food back to their respective holes in the sand. For some reason, they would drop their breakfast outside before entering their home. After a few moments, each would return for their food and go back inside to eat. No sand wasp ever deviated from this behavior.

Apparently, over the centuries, natural selection favored sand wasps with two survival-programs: 1) never eat outside, and 2) always check for intruders before bringing food inside to eat. Both of these survival-programs decreased the chance of sand wasps being eaten by a predator, and therefore increased the chances for the survival of the species.

The scientists decided to find out just how firmly this program was ingrained. They observed a sand wasp with a dead horsefly. When it left its food next to the entrance of its hole to check inside, the scientists moved the horsefly a couple of feet away.

The sand wasp returned to get its breakfast and, of course, found nothing. It began to look for food, just as if it never had it in the first place. After a few minutes, the sand wasp found the same horsefly and proceeded to drag it back to its hole, leave it, and again go inside to look for intruders.

Again, the scientists moved the horsefly while the sand wasp was gone. When it returned to find its food missing, the sand wasp began to search for food again – and again – and again.

The scientists kept repeating this experiment, always with the same results. Eventually the sand wasp died of exhaustion and starvation, literally with food in its mouth. The scientists surmised the sand wasp was incapable of changing its survival-program, even when circumstances had turned it into a non-survival program.

Moral

A great many sand wasps are disguised as people…

doing the same thing over and over again,

even if it isn't doing them any good.

Even if it is killing them.

Non-Survival Programs

People may be ignorant, but they are not stupid. There is always some value to a fear-based reaction. Otherwise, this type of behavior would never be repeated often enough to become a conscious pre-action – and, ultimately, an unconscious survival program.

> **While Survival Programs always have some value,**
> **they are only valuable in the specific situations**
> **for which they were created.**

Since they are unconscious, survival programs can lose effectiveness, and even become invitations to disaster, when circumstances change. For example, *"Look both ways before you cross the street"* is a common admonition by parents who are trying to create safe behavior in their children. Typically, this warning occurs so often that it becomes an automatic survival program, needing no thought whatsoever. Eventually, it occurs when the act is unnecessary. In fact, most adults probably look both ways even when crossing a one-way street.

However, just as with the Sand Wasp, even the survival program of looking both ways before crossing the street has the potential of becoming a non-survival program capable of causing injury and death. It almost happened to me.

On my first trip to New Zealand, I was almost run over as I crossed the street. As is my survival program, I automatically looked to the left to check the road in the direction I am used to the traffic coming from. Unfortunately for me, in New Zealand the traffic travels in the opposite direction.

Seeing it was all clear to the left, I stepped off the curb an instant before I looked to the right … where the traffic was actually coming from. Oops. Fortunately, a wonderfully alert friend pulled me back just as I was about to be flattened by a bus. My survival program, which had served me in the USA, did not serve me in New Zealand. It had become a non-survival program, because it had me look the wrong way first.

In the earlier example, the little boy developed a survival program of withholding his feelings. This behavior clearly protected him, because it placated his father.

The little boy grew up, got a job, and got married – but retained his unconscious survival program of withholding his feelings. This created a strain on both his career and his marriage. He had difficulty sharing his ideas at work, and could not open up with his wife at all.

He did not succeed to his potential in the workplace, because he was afraid to risk the rejection of his ideas. This man also failed to succeed in his marriage, as his frustrated spouse divorced him because he was emotionally unavailable to her. The fear-based survival program, which once served the child, did not serve the adult. His survival program had become a non-survival program.

Three Classic Survival Programs

1) ***"Don't talk to strangers"*** is a classic survival program that can protect children from harm. However, it often shifts from a survival to non-survival program later in life. When your boss tells you to go and find new clients he or she might as well say, ***"Go talk to strangers."***

2) ***"Eat everything on your plate"*** is another common survival program. Following this instruction eliminates ridicule and punishment at meals. However, it goes from a survival program to a non-survival program years later when you have a weight problem … and are not able to leave the table if any food is remaining on your plate, even when you have had enough to eat.

3) ***"Children should be seen and not heard"*** and ***"Don't speak unless spoken to"*** are survival programs that can keep children from being punished in social situations. They become non-survival programs when low self-worth and anxiety prevent successful personal and professional relationships.

A valuable survival program in one environment can easily become a destructive non-survival program in another. Once a survival program becomes a non-survival program, it will continue to be self-destructive until you change your behavior. Unfortunately, most of us make excuses instead of changing.

"I'm sorry. I haven't slept in two days."

"Of course I'm mad. You broke your promise to me."

"It wasn't my fault. He cut me off."

"I'm only yelling at you because you're yelling at me!"

"I'm overwhelmed. I don't mean to be taking it out on you."

"If you had a childhood like mine, you'd be messed-up too."

and my personal favorite: *"I'm only human."*

Do any of these excuses sound familiar?

Most people are their own worst enemy. They continue demonstrating behaviors long after the situation for which they created the behavior has ended ... thus creating a non-survival program.

Many people continue to demonstrate non-survival programs even after they have become aware of the problems those programs are creating (such as smoking, violence, unworthiness, shyness, arrogance, and so on). Whether conscious or unconscious, these programs sabotage personal and professional results. Furthermore, the negative results will continue until there is a conscious choice to change the behavior.

"If you always do what you've always done,

you'll always get what you've always got."

Various Sources

In other words, if you want to get something different, you have to do something different. Unfortunately, the normal reaction to change is to resist it. Even when the old benefits are gone, the program often remains. Benjamin Franklin reportedly fought this tendency by changing a habit every 21 days. Interestingly, two centuries later, Maxwell Maltz showed in his book, *Psychocybernetics*, that it takes 21 days to change a habit.

One of the great myths is, *"Mistakes are just learning experiences."* Nonsense; mistakes are NOT learning experiences ... unless you actually learn something from them and make changes. By continuing old survival programs that have become non-productive, negative, or even destructive, you only succeed in cementing the guarantee that nothing will ever change.

In what ways have you become your own worst enemy,
with Survival Programs that have become non-productive,
negative, or even destructive Non-Survival Programs?

Fortunately, we are not sand wasps. Human beings have the ability to evaluate their circumstances and do things differently. Herein is our ability to develop leadership excellence.

The Three Levels of Negative Circumstances

Despite the fact that all negative reactions are fear-based, fear is not the issue. Fear is valuable; it can keep us alive when there is danger. The real problem is the negative, non-productive, or destructive behaviors that can be triggered by even a small level of fear.

Negative circumstances do not cause fear-based reactions, but they are used to justify them. When you react to being hurt, or pre-act to the possibility of being hurt, you blame others for your fear-based reactions. For example, *"I wouldn't have yelled at you if you hadn't yelled at me."*

The Three Levels of Negative Circumstances

Level 1:   DISTRACTION

Level 2:   DAMAGE

Level 3:   DEATH

Fear-based reactions are rationalized, even if afterwards you wish you had behaved differently. You may say, *"I can't believe I yelled at her,"* but you rationalized it anyway, perhaps because you were frustrated. At other times you might think, *"I should have ripped his lungs out,"* but you either justified withholding your anger to protect this person, or to protect yourself.

Negative circumstances do not cause fear-based reactions. If they did, we would all react in the same way when faced with a similar event, and we would do so every time. Yes, people have habits and tendencies, but nobody acts the same way all of the time.

Consider child abuse. It has been said that all child abusers were abused as children. Those who know the horror of it are the ones who pass it on to others. For these people, the problem has evolved from being abused by others, to one of being abusive to others.

Yet not all abused children become abusers. For some people, the negative circumstance of abuse has created new problems. They have become inward, fearful, shy, distant and avoidant.

However, there are people who have been abused who have become neither abusive nor avoidant. These are the ones who now strive to help others. Often, they become counselors for other victims of abuse. Sometimes, they even become counselors for abusers. I have met many such people. Their power is awesome.

As destructive as child abuse is, the circumstance of abuse is not the real issue for adult survivors. Their true problems are the fear-based reactions they have developed as a result of the abuse. Ultimately, it will be whether they choose to overcome these behaviors which will determine how successful they will become as adults.

There are no guarantees. When you choose to strive for solutions to problems, others may still choose to react. If that is the case, however, you really have not lost anything. Anyone who reacts negatively to positive suggestions would have most likely been negative regardless of your actions. By taking the higher road, you create a chance for positive results, and those results can be amazing.

I have heard stories of hurt ranging from minor to deadly. Not surprisingly, the most intense reaction to hurtful situations is hatred. However, since hate is an intensely unpleasant emotion, many people will resist sharing or even acknowledging personal hurtful experiences. Unfortunately, just as a cancer you ignore remains deadly, the hate you bury is still destructive.

I have often said, *"However hurtful the event; hate is a choice. Hurt does not cause hate. You can make other choices."* Reactions to this statement have ranged from confusion to angry disbelief.

For example, I have six children. I have been blessed to be present at each birth. During labor, I watched my wife's pain of childbirth increase to levels incomprehensible to me. However, when the big moment finally arrived, I observed a wave of peace and unlimited love for the child whose birth caused the extreme pain that still gives me shivers. I doubt any male can truly comprehend the experience.

If hurt caused hate, all mothers would loathe their newborns. In reality, many women go from agony to serenity just moments after giving birth. Most women would call the police if a man caused them one-tenth of the pain they experienced in childbirth, and they would resent him for decades.

"Now ladies," I ask my students, *"if a man were causing you this level of pain, would you be filled with joy and peace, just because he stopped? Relief, perhaps. But joy?"*

Depending on the group, if they do not laugh, they simply frown and shake their heads and say, *"No."* They know, of course, that in childbirth, peace does not occur simply because the pain stops. Indeed, the pain often continues. There is peace because something significant was accomplished.

Conversely, pain without a meaningful purpose is just suffering. Peace and joy do not follow, resentment does. *"You hurt me and I hate you!"* However, by hating, you suffer even more.

Many times I have said, *"If you hate someone, who has the hate?"*

"I do," is the typical response.

Then I ask, *"What's that hate doing to you?"*

Many people have rationalized and avoided a truthful answer. But eventually, each would look at me and say, *"It's killing me, Ross."*

> *"Hating someone is like taking rat poison, and expecting the other person to die."*
>
> A participant in one of my seminars

59

Level-3 Negative Circumstance: DEATH

There is nothing more challenging to human beings than facing death. While some of us have more experiences with death than others, all of us will have at least our own death to deal with. Many people spend a lifetime in terror of dying. Nevertheless, if you are consumed with fears of death you cannot truly live.

We are often overwhelmed with the passing of loved ones. We are also affected by the deaths of strangers, especially when it feels unjust. This was clearly demonstrated by the attacks on the World Trade Center and the Pentagon. Billions of people, not just friends, relatives, and acquaintances of the victims, felt a deep personal loss.

Level-3 Negative Circumstances often inspire "eye-for-an-eye" reactions, as well as possible escalations. One drive-by shooting is invariably followed by another. Convicted murderers may face the death penalty. A bombing in Northern Ireland only serves to justify a bloody retaliation. The United States invaded Afghanistan and Iraq following the attacks of September 11, 2001.

"An eye for an eye for an eye for an eye ...
ends in making everybody blind."

Mahatma Gandhi

"The old law of an eye for an eye leaves everyone blind."

Dr. Martin Luther King Jr.

Leo Buscaglia (the former "Love 101" professor at the University of Southern California, hugging activist, PBS personality, and author of the book, *"Love"*) viewed death as an inevitability, and said that we should stop being consumed with it and enjoy life. He used to joke about death in an attempt to reduce people's fear of it. At an address at the University of Illinois he mused, *"We are trapped! None of us will ever get off this planet alive!"*

Level-2 Negative Circumstance: DAMAGE

Level-2 Negative Circumstances involve damage or destruction. Examples could include being passed over for a promotion, having a house fire, being involved in a car accident, being audited, getting mugged, having an idea stolen, breaking off an engagement, being physically or sexually abused, getting fired, going to jail, losing the value in a retirement account, getting a divorce, going bankrupt, or breaking an arm.

Regardless of how bad a Level-2 Negative Circumstance might be, at least you survived. Yet, many of us have seen people react so strongly that they have turned a Level-2 difficulty into a Level-3 disaster. A simple fender-bender often triggers road rage, which sometimes escalates into a fatal *second* collision. A disgruntled employee loses his job, then returns to shoot his boss, or other employees. In a bad economy, people have committed suicide after losing money on their investments.

> *"That which does not kill me makes me stronger."*
>
> Friedrich Nietzsche

The problem is not what triggers your negative reactions. The problem is that your negative reactions are "trigger-able".

No matter how much you feel justified to react negatively, it rarely creates success or peace in the long run. Reacting to a Level-2 Negative Circumstance often makes a bad situation much worse. In fact, it was his fear-based reactions to an incorrect perception of a Level-2 Negative Circumstance, which led George to make choices that were destructive to himself and everything he loved.

More importantly, when you choose to lead with love in a Level-2 Negative Circumstance there is always a benefit. Always. Even if the only benefit is to your blood-pressure.

Face it, fear-based reactions to Level-2 Negative Circumstances tend to escalate. Think of the minimal damage Friendly Fred caused to the Cadillac, which escalated when my father damaged Fred's lawn, sprinkler and draperies.

Fred owned guns. I shudder to think where this escalation of fear-based reactions could have ended, had my mother not turned Friendly Fred and my father around with a simple love-based gift of flowers and a note. I wonder what George could have created if he had chosen to lead with love?

Level-1 Negative Circumstance: DISTRACTION

Now we come to Level 1, by far the most common negative circumstances. They include irritations, inconveniences, and unwanted surprises, such as having a bad waiter or being stuck in traffic. Other examples could include having a critical spouse, getting laughed at, having a bad hair day, missing a big sale, or your kids spilling their milk.

Reacting to Level-1 Negative Circumstances always makes you "smaller". Or, as my father said on the Thursday night of my first LifeStream seminar in 1975 (page 11), *"You are only as big as the smallest thing it takes to upset you."*

Have you ever yelled at someone who was yelling at you? Did you ever gossip about someone who had an affair? How about lying to someone who lied to you, or shutting someone out because he or she annoyed you? Then there is my favorite, have you ever pretended that things are "Fine. Just fine," when you actually feel hurt and angry?

> **A Fear-Based Reactor focuses on the REASON he or she is reacting.**
>
> **A Love-Based Leader focuses on the FACT he or she is reacting at all.**

Have you ever gotten angry with someone who cut you off, because they just missed colliding with your car? In reality, they missed you. There was no accident (which would have been a Level-2 Negative Circumstance) and no one died (a Level-3 Negative Circumstance). Isn't NOT getting hit by another car a good thing? Nevertheless, there are many stories of road rage escalating similar Level-1 negative circumstances into manslaughter (Level-3). They did not even need a fender-bender to justify it. *"You almost hit me"* was enough of an excuse.

When you are reacting negatively to a relatively small problem, you are usually hurting yourself more than the problem did. There is only one way to handle Level-1 Negative Circumstances, and that is to "Get Over Yourself" (which also helps with Level-2 and Level-3).

"Get Over Yourself" is much more than just a cute phrase or a negative put-down. I have used this expression to define a concept that has helped thousands of people to improve their results in life. People see their health, attitude, relationships, and leadership effectiveness increase when they stop taking themselves too seriously. In fact, I have seen seminar participants create miraculous new circumstances in their lives by using the concepts and tools presented in my *"Get Over Yourself"* CDs and seminars.

Everyone will face Level-1 Negative Circumstances on a daily basis. Quit letting the small stuff push your buttons. Do not turn your mole-hills into mountains. It is time to stop reacting negatively, and to instead learn to laugh at yourself. If you do not "Get Over Yourself," you will be giving your power away to every little thing that goes wrong.

The Reactive Cycle

Whether you are overwhelmed by fears, or are in denial of fears, the real problem remains the same. It is not the negative circumstances that need addressing, but rather your fear-based reactions to them.

Not only do your fear-based reactions create their own negative circumstances for you, they also automatically become the negative circumstances for other people. You are reacting because they are reacting. They are reacting because you are reacting. Once begun, this cycle is extremely difficult to stop and it usually escalates.

Let us say you make the statement, *"I wouldn't have yelled at you, if you hadn't yelled at me."* Then the other person argues, *"Well, I wouldn't have yelled at you, if you had kept your promise"* (or something similar). Justifications for fear-based reactions are easy to come by.

When everyone blames everyone else for his or her own negativity, nobody is in charge. This is when damage occurs. Sometimes the damage is major.

While undesired situations often trigger your fear-based reactions, they do not cause them. Your negative circumstances are simply the excuses. They then become the excuses for other people's fear-based reactions in return. Once initiated, continued negativity accelerates this cycle.

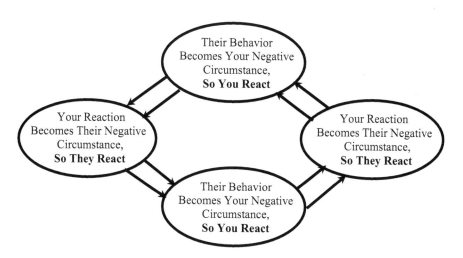

When you are in The Reactive Cycle, and demonstrating any of the four fear-based reactions (Fight, Flight, Freeze or Facade), you literally become a "Victim of Circumstances".

<u>Overcoming Fear-Based Reactions</u>

You cannot overcome fear-based reactions, pre-actions, or non-survival programs, unless you know they exist. On the other hand, you will not overcome them, unless you see them as a problem. Even then, you have to learn how.

The Definition of Insanity:

"Doing the same thing over and over again,

and expecting different results."

Attributed to Benjamin Franklin, Mark Twain, Albert Einstein, and mystery writer Rita Mae Brown in her novel *Sudden Death.*

A middle-aged woman in a wheelchair told me the story of her crippling injury. She had been a high school teacher. During a fire drill, it was her job to see that everyone left the building as quickly as possible. A large student walked toward her, and she told him he needed to go outside. He said he wanted his jacket. Since it was not cold, she insisted that he wait to get his coat until after the drill. The young man became so enraged that he threw her against a wall of lockers. Not only did this cripple her, but it put the young man in prison.

Who knows for sure what caused this non-survival behavior. Perhaps anger helped him to survive an abusive parent, but there was certainly some reason it developed. Apparently, he perceived the ability to intimidate people as valuable, even though it caused grave injury to them and ultimately ruined his life. Violent people might loathe the consequences of their behavior, but they continue to react with intense rage because of perceived benefits associated with the ability to intimidate and control others.

Anger is not the only way people go about trying to control others. In elementary school, I recall a girl struggling to answer a question from our teacher. Instead of answering, she began to tremble and cry. The teacher became visibly nervous and told her to sit down, where she continued to whimper. I cannot remember this girl ever being asked another question.

Falling apart had an immediate benefit for the young girl. She did not have to answer the question. It also had a long-term benefit. The teacher never called on her again. Shy people are not stupid. Even if they hate themselves for not speaking up, they often stay silent because of the inherent value in being able to avoid ridicule, rejection, or perhaps embarrassment.

These two young people had something in common with each other. Their fear-based reactions had become their ways of controlling others. The tough kid accomplished this with his FIGHT reaction, and the young girl with her FREEZE reaction.

That is certainly not all. We have all known people who have learned to use the FACADE reaction to control others with untruths, half-truths, and outright lies. Almost everyone has encountered people who resort to the FLIGHT reaction … people who quit jobs if they think they are in trouble, or who are always the one to initiate the break-up of a relationship. The trick, instead of justifying fear-based reactions, is to overcome them.

Our perceptions of the value of our fear-based reactions may blind us to the problems they are creating in our lives. We insist that others should do the changing, while going to great lengths to justify our own Fight, Flight, Freeze, and Facade reactions … even when they only serve to make things worse.

Your fear-based reactions usually do you harm, if only because they give others an excuse to react in turn. So even when you win you lose. People who back off from your intimidation may actively work to undermine you to get even. Your shyness may evoke sympathy from those who care about you, but bosses who think you are too fragile to handle more responsibility may pass you over for a promotion.

The normal reaction to change is resistance, even when you see a need to make the change. But it is virtually impossible to change a behavior when you do not see a need to make the change … even if it is ruining your life. A classic example is the practicing alcoholic who says, *"Drinking is not my problem. My crummy job is the problem."*

There are only two ways your life can improve.

1) Everyone else changes how they are treating you.

2) You change how you are treating everyone else.

Becoming familiar with your own fear-based reactions will not guarantee that you will overcome them, but it is the first step. However, such awareness is necessary for you to increase your leadership effectiveness and thus avoid taking "The Fear-Based Path of Self-Sabotage" (Page 66).

While you will find in the coming chapters that the path of *The Love-Based Leader* is a terrific alternative, it is important for you to be clear on knowing "where you are", before you spend effort striving to get "where you want to be". Therefore, I strongly recommend that you spend a few minutes on the following exercise before you continue on to Part II.

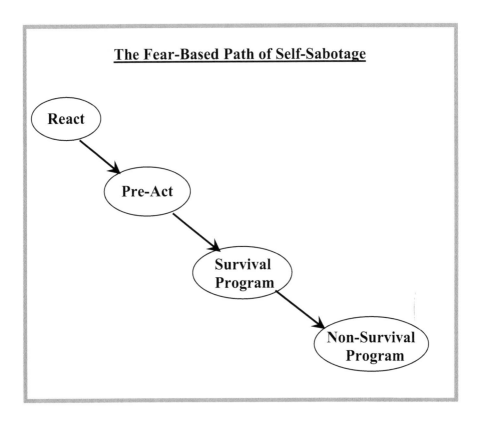

The Fear-Based Path of Self-Sabotage

React

Pre-Act

Survival Program

Non-Survival Program

EXERCISE #2 - Your Non-Survival Programs

Non-survival programs, by definition, are unconscious fear-based behaviors. Changing them is impossible unless you discover what they are. Here are two ways you can uncover your non-survival programs:

1) Have you ever done something, regretted it — but later did it again? List a few examples:

_____

_____

_____

_____

_____

_____

_____

2) Have you ever avoided doing something, and regretted it — but when given another chance avoided it again? List a few examples:

_____

_____

_____

_____

_____

_____

_____

Love-Based Leadership:

The process of making a positive difference,

and inspiring others to do the same,

by maintaining self-control.

PART II
THE SOLUTION

Love-Based Leadership

Leadership based on "Position-Power" is history.

It is time to stop fighting against what you do not want,
and to start fighting for what you do want.

There is a difference.

This is the essence of *Love-Based Leadership.*
Its time has come.

CHAPTER 3

Who Wants to WORK on a Relationship?

For the past 30 years, when speaking to groups about relationships, I have asked them this question. *"Raise your hand if you know a lot of people who have great relationships."* I never see very many hands.

To be certain, many of the people in my audiences have had great relationships themselves, and most knew at least a few people with great relationships. Nevertheless, very few knew many others who had them.

Today we find many competent people are failing to excel, or even to survive in their personal and professional relationships because they lack "relationship" skills. They fail because they leave the development and maintenance of trusting relationships to chance.

Everywhere I go, people say to me, "We are working on our relationship." Who wants to "work" on a relationship? I love to ask them if working on the relationship is what drew them to each other? Normally, relationships begin because there is joy at some level. In my experience, relationships begin to deteriorate when they become "serious".

Do you really want to be in a "serious" relationship?

Most people would rather be right than happy.
The truth is that seriousness is a "disease".

Fortunately, it is curable.

We live in a world where a properly focused person can create virtually anything they want, perhaps not everything they want, but almost anything is within reach of a committed individual. Nevertheless, the one thing missing is what people seem to want the most: A great relationship.

Some people have great models for personal relationships in their parents, but many do not. While it is understandable to have difficulty creating great relationships without a great model, it is not exactly easy to accomplish this even with a great model. I grew up in one of the happiest households imaginable, yet my parents divorced after 35 years of marriage. Additionally, my brother, my sister and I have all been divorced.

Roberta Rockefeller and Me

I met Roberta Rockefeller while attending the University of Southern California. We were inseparable. We were lovers and best friends. Shortly after I graduated, we got married.

Roberta and I lived in Los Angeles, and each had our own convertible sports car. We had good jobs, spent a lot of time at the beach, and had many friends. Not only were Roberta and I on "The Newlywed Game", we won. We really did have a great life together.

After three years of marriage, we decided to have children. Roberta gave birth to Kelcey, the first of our three daughters. Jancy and Carly followed two and four years later. I was the proud papa of three beautiful, healthy, intelligent girls.

We should have been the picture of joy. However, we were not happy.

Roberta had wanted children since she was a child. Roberta's feelings for our daughters were more important than her need for my friendship. She did not ignore me after they were born; I simply stopped being her best friend. In retrospect, I do not think my ego ever allowed me to be anything other than Roberta's best friend.

I always had a fear of divorce. My parents had been married for decades, as had Roberta's. I actually had made the commitment to never do anything "wrong". If there were ever to be a divorce, it would not be my fault. Accordingly, I never had an affair, never used drugs, and never got drunk. There were no beatings, expensive hobbies, or gambling. I worked hard, earned a good living, and provided a nice home for my family. I never did anything wrong (I hope you can see what is coming).

All relationships have problems. I, of course, never did anything wrong. Therefore, who had to be causing all the problems? Correct, Roberta was clearly the problem. Surely, you can see that? (Yes, this is sarcasm). It still amazes me that she was able to put up with such self-righteousness for 10 years. Obviously, she loved me a lot.

Nevertheless, I became critical, offensive, and judgmental of practically everything Roberta did, or did not do. I may not have been happy, but it certainly was *"not my fault."*

72

In retrospect, I try to imagine what it must have been like living with me. I really cannot.

Finally, she had had enough. Ours was one of the first "No-Fault" divorces in Illinois. It only cost a few hundred dollars, and we were only in court for about 15 minutes (at least we did that part right).

Roberta rented a house about 45 minutes away from where I lived. I only saw my daughters on alternate weekends, a couple of weeks over the summer, plus a few days over the Christmas holidays. I felt like an uncle.

Residual resentment from 10 years of marriage, along with current resentments resulting from being divorced, welled up inside of me. I hated paying child support, and I loathed hearing good or bad news about my daughters over the phone. Not surprisingly, I began to resist my divorce and to avoid keeping my commitments to her and my daughters.

For example, I would show up a few minutes late every time I picked up the girls. Then, depending on which would be more inconvenient for Roberta, I would either drop them off a little early, or a bit late. I would do anything I could to make her life more difficult.

My resistance peaked when I began to manipulate the child support payments. I had agreed to pay child support every week, and of course I continued to never do anything "wrong" (self-righteousness is a non-survival program). I mailed each check on a Friday, so it would be post-marked before the deadline, but would not arrive until Monday or Tuesday. This, of course, was not my fault.

Roberta finally got really angry with me, so I told her she would get her checks by Saturday if I had to drive them to her house. I would ruin my own weekend by driving the check to her home and leaving it stuck in the door about one minute before midnight (what a jerk I was).

Finally, after about 18 months of this nonsense, I got it. I really got it. I finally saw what I was doing. I still remember the feeling as I was writing a child-support check. I stopped as it hit me. *"You know,"* I thought, *"this is a lot of money. But, she used to get all of it. Now, I get to keep most of it."* I smiled, and everything changed.

> **Suddenly, my attitude changed completely.**
>
> **Life the way it "is" became better than life the way it "isn't".**

I even had the thought, *"Besides, if I had to pay someone to take care of my daughters as well as Roberta does, I would never be able to afford it. Heck, this is actually pretty reasonable."*

It was then that I remembered my commitment to Roberta. When we got married, I made a promise before God, my family, and our friends to *"Love, honor, and cherish"* her *"until death do us part."* I had not made that commitment conditionally on how Roberta would treat me. I said I would cherish

Roberta until I died. I swore an oath to that.

I never realized until that moment, the reason Roberta divorced me was because I destroyed the trust and the love. I finally realized that I bastardized my own integrity the first time I criticized her instead of cherishing her (I probably did that on our wedding day).

Over the years, I gave her countless reasons to distrust me. From Roberta's perspective, if I had lied about committing to cherish her *"until death do us part,"* then it was certainly possible that I had lied about loving her as well.

Roberta asked for the divorce, that much is true. However, I was the one who ended our marriage when I showed I could not be trusted.

I called Roberta and asked her if it would be OK if I would send her four checks at the beginning of every month, each post-dated for its respective Saturday. That way, I explained, she would never have to worry about when they would show up. She almost fainted. I finally started to see that cherishing Roberta again was going to be fun.

The effects of this change on my part were staggering.

I finally stopped living with resentment.

That alone was worth my efforts. But when Roberta started encouraging our daughters to spend more time with me, I actually started to live in joy again.

Then, I got a lesson I was not expecting. I never realized how my anger for Roberta was affecting how other women perceived me. Within weeks of changing my attitude about Roberta, the incredible Christine Gail Lesch entered my life.

My divorce, which had been my curse, had now become my blessing. Because Roberta had divorced me, I was now free to create an even better relationship with someone I would have been too unworthy to even consider dating when I was younger. Fortunately, for me, Christine and I were married later that same year.

To see just how much healing occurred, a few years later when Roberta and Harry Begley were about to be married, Christine and I were invited to their wedding. That may be common in some parts of the world (I am kidding), but it is rare in Chicago.

Harry and I even posed for a photo to commemorate the last moment that, *"Neither one of us are married to Roberta."* However, what made me most proud is that Roberta asked my wife Christine to sing at her ceremony. That was pure class.

However, having a wife and a former wife who get along with each other does create some interesting moments. Such as the time I heard them trading stories about me, and laughing hysterically.

Nevertheless, I would not trade our friendship for anything. Roberta has helped us out of two financial binds, and she was with my father when he died.

Roberta is still one of my best friends.

I cannot take credit for our friendship, as we both created that. All I did was stop resenting, start giving, and allow her to give to me.

My decision to keep my integrity has inspired numerous seminar participants to give their marriage a second chance. I have also been told that this story has helped many people re-create friendships after a bitter break-up ... just as Roberta and I did.

Roberta's Response

Shortly after finishing the "Roberta and Me" section of this chapter, I sent it to Roberta. I wanted to make sure I was objective and not judgmental. I wanted to make certain it did not cause new resentments on her part. I was so moved by her response that I asked for, and received, her permission to include it in the book.

Hi Ross,

I have just finished reading the section about you and me. I am deeply touched. Thank you. I wouldn't change a word.

Perhaps someday I'll share my version of our story with you. However, I am guessing you already know a lot of it. I will always love you, and I do cherish you and all that we have shared. Most of all our friendship and our daughters.

Christine and your children rank high on my list, too. Not to mention your family.

And then there are all the memories. I basically grew up with you, most of my memories include you, and most of the funny stories I tell involve you. I have many "Ross-isms" that are cherished parts of me.

Most of all, I manage to make sure that just about everyone I meet, and have an intimate conversation with, knows that I am blessed to have an exceptional relationship with my first husband, his wife, their children, and the rest of his family.

Love Roberta

RELATING

What is a relationship anyway? A "relationship" is a noun. Dictionaries describe a relationship as, "a connection, association, or involvement that people have with other individuals or groups."

Everyone has relationships. We have personal relationships, intimate relationships, family relationships, work relationships, and community relationships. We have joyful relationships with people we love and difficult relationships with people we resent. We even have temporary relationships with the other drivers on the highway, the rest of the audience in a play, and the people who join us on a flight or in an elevator.

However brief, the existence of a relationship has nothing to do with its depth, longevity, quality, or your desire to maintain or improve it. That is up to you.

Relating, on the other hand, is what determines the effectiveness of our relationships. The word "relate" is a verb. It is an action. The dictionary definition of "relate" is, "to have a friendly or close relationship with another, or others ... to be responsive or sympathetic."

Do not try to MAKE a relationship work.
Instead, simply strive to RELATE.

Stress is a normal result of personal, intimate, and business relationships. The common denominator in all of our lives is that we must relate with people when there are problems and conflicts. So why are we usually able to relate with some people, but rarely with certain others?

The answer is directly proportional to the existence of mutual trust. While we would prefer to relate with people we trust, situations often require us to relate with people when trust is lacking.

There is a quandary whenever you decide to trust another person. Regardless of the potential benefits, you become open to the possibility of being hurt. On the other hand, when you do not trust, regardless of the hurt you may avoid, you guarantee lost opportunities for the achievement of desired results that could have been created, such as success, love, friendship, and self-worth.

It is easy to create an atmosphere in which you are not trusted. Simply break your word, show up late, gossip, judge, attack, lie, cheat, or violate confidences enough times and even profoundly valuable professional and personal relationships can be ruined. With some people, even one time is enough to break the trust. Once gone, regaining trust is usually difficult and often impossible.

In both business and personal relationships, if you gain an advantage over others by abusing trust, there is always a cost. Not the least of which is a guarantee that the advantage cannot be sustained. If your behavior threatens others, ultimately they will react to you in one of four ways. They will attack you, leave you, shut you out, lie to you, or some combination thereof. Are any of these possible negative reactions truly in your best interest?

In business, ethics demand you keep your word to employees, employers, co-workers, and clients. Regardless of the reasons, if your behavior causes others to lose trust in you, you lose.

Many people resist giving when they take a job. Instead of exceeding expectations, they give just enough to keep from getting fired. This is probably fair, since these types of people seem to end up working for bosses who only pay their employees just enough to keep them from quitting. Everyone is worried about what they are going to get, instead of concentrating on what they have to give. With so many adversarial relationships, it is no wonder so many businesses are failing.

The same is true with personal relationships. Some people get married then seem to look for excuses to stop giving. They do not mean it when they say, *"I promise to love, honor, and cherish until death do us part."* They might as well just say, *"I promise to tolerate you until I feel like killing you."*

You have probably heard the old saying, *"It takes two people to make a relationship work."* This is incorrect. It does not take two people to make a relationship work. But it does takes two to destroy one.

It actually only takes one person to make a relationship work. Furthermore, you have always known this. You have just believed it was the "other" one.

Once people begin to take it personally when something goes wrong, they begin to resent their partner for the smallest of challenges, and the Reactive Cycle begins. Once begun, this can be a very difficult thing to stop.

In every relationship, there exist many Level-1 negative circumstances (Distractions), such as finding the toilet seat being left up at home, or make-up scattered all over the counter. Even mild fear-based reactions to these events, such as arguing and sarcasm, can easily create much bigger problems.

When a relationship ends, there are always excuses and accusations. Usually, both people end up claiming the fault lies in the other person. However, neither one ever seems to blame the real culprit: Their own fear-based reactions to Level-1 Negative Circumstances. These are what really lead most partners to begin withholding love from each other.

Imagine, for example, a spouse who consistently leaves the cap off the toothpaste tube. Instead of allowing a fear-based reaction, a love-based leader makes a conscious choice to keep their word to "cherish" the growing glob of toothpaste on their counter. They may also choose to buy a second tube for their own use, and hide it out of arm's reach.

The love-based spouse keeps the promise, *"to love, honor, and cherish until death do us part,"* regardless of the issues and problems. He or she finds a way to enjoy their partner's little quirks. They maintain their integrity and honor their promise to cherish, no matter what it takes.

Who wants to "work" on a relationship anyway? True answers will almost always be found through joy. What "Level -1 Negative Circumstances" generally cause you to react? What are those negative reactions doing to your relationships?

"I Haven't Spoken To My Mother In 20 years."

It was Sunday of another LifeStream Basic Seminar. The breakthroughs and insights were typically profound. "Joan" came to the front of the room and shared, *"I haven't spoken to my mother in 20 years."*

She and her mother had fought over how she was raising her children. It was a bitter argument. Joan was so tired of fighting she finally told her mother, *"I never want to speak to you again."*

My father asked Joan what she wanted. Her response was simple. *"I want my mother back."*

He told Joan, *"Go call her."*

While everyone else took a break, I accompanied her to the pay phones. Joan was shaking so severely she could barely dial the phone. It took a few minutes to connect, but when I heard the words, *"Mother it's me, Joan."* I stepped away to give her privacy. She was already sobbing.

Later, when Joan returned to the room, it was clear she was excited. Her smile went practically from ear to ear. Joan shared with us that she and her mother had cried together for the last 25 minutes, and had shared regret and longing which both had been carrying for years. Joan had made a commitment to visit her mother the following weekend. She was glowing.

About 20 other people were so moved by Joan, that they all called their parents or children during that lunch break. It was an inspiring afternoon. Joan's courage affected people she would never meet. It was a terrific example of the impact of *The Love-Based Leader* in action.

Later, Joan told us about the wonderful weekend she and her mother had shared. They visited, shopped, and toured Indianapolis together. One time they began crying and hugging while crossing the street. The light changed during their hug and a police officer actually had to move them to the curb. It must have been like a scene from a movie.

Several days later, her mother was killed in an automobile accident. I saw Joan before she left for the funeral. I was amazed. She was completely at peace. Joan told me that, had she not reconciled with her mother, the accident would have probably killed her as well. Now, she could let her mother go. At the funeral, Joan re-connected with a few other long-lost relatives. Today, she no longer lives in isolation.

Who Have You Lost Touch With?

This Is A Wonderful Opportunity For You

To Experience *Love-Based Leadership*.

Giving Unconditionally

Throughout history, only a handful of people have spent their lives giving love unconditionally ... giving without a thought of anything in return. Unfortunately, once you get past people such as Jesus Christ, Mahatma Gandhi, Mother Teresa, Dr. Martin Luther King, Jr., Dr Albert Schweitzer and a few others, the list drops off rather quickly.

Most of us are not so good at giving unconditionally. We typically give with conditions ...

Conditional Giving

At Home

"I'll love you IF you love me back."

"I'll love you UNLESS you fool around."

"I'll love you UNTIL you hurt me."

At Work

"I'll work hard IF you give me a raise."

"I won't quit UNLESS you take advantage of me."

"I'll be loyal UNTIL you stop promoting me."

Then, when the other person does not meet your conditions, you have justification to withhold your love in a relationship, or your passion at work. When your giving is done "conditionally", it is really not giving at all. It is actually an attempt to manipulate or control others, and it is exhausting.

Giving, true unconditional giving, is energizing. If you really want inner peace, quality relationships, and a successful career, quit focusing on what you are going to get. Instead focus on what you are going to give.

When I make that statement in my seminars, I often hear someone remark *"I gave until I was used up,"* or *"I gave until I could give no more."* These are well-worn justifications for giving up on a relationship or a job. These and other similar comments indicate that it was the giving that drained the individual. This is untrue, and I can prove it.

Think back to a time when you were shopping for a gift for a dear friend, and you found the perfect gift. You know, the kind of gift that was so perfect, you could not wait to see the expression on the face of the receiver?

You took it home and wrapped it with feelings of joy and anticipation. Then, when the gifts were being opened, you casually kept pushing it back out of the way until it was the last gift. Remember how you felt as you commented, *"Oh, here is one more gift."* Your smile was so big your friend knew something was up, and perhaps even looked at you and said, *"OK, what are you up to?"* as they opened their gift.

Now recall the gasp, scream, or laugh when your friend opened the package and said, *"Where did you find this, I can't believe it. It's just perfect!"* Rather than being drained or exhausted, you were energized, weren't you? You were smiling, laughing, crying, hugging, joyful, and excited. Giving always creates energy.

Years later, long after you forgot what you received that day, you still remember the moment he or she opened your gift. You have always known the truth: The gift is in the giving.

"It isn't what you do, it's how much love you put in the doing.

It isn't what you give, it's how much love you put in the giving."

Mother Teresa

Mother Teresa created peace and joy in Calcutta. You and I have created turmoil at birthday parties and vacations. The question is, could we do better?

All of us have experienced giving or receiving unconditional love. Granted, some of us have experienced more than others, but we have all experienced at least some.

"Love in your heart wasn't put there to stay.

Love isn't love until you give it away"

Unknown

In your career, have you ever screwed up, but been given a second chance? Perhaps you forgave a friend for hurting you not because they treated you badly, but in spite of that fact. Maybe a fatigued parent chose to stay up all night caring for you when you were sick, despite needing sleep.

EXERCISE #3 - The Highest Blessing

Most people are familiar with this quote from the Bible. *"It is more blessed to give than to receive."* (Acts 20:35)

QUESTION:

If it really is, *"more blessed to give than to receive,"* then what is the highest thing you can do for another human being?

ANSWER:

_____

_____

_____

_____

<< PLEASE: ANSWER BEFORE CONTINUING ... NO CHEATING!! >>

- -

When asked the question, *"If it really is more blessed to give than to receive, then what is the highest thing you can do for another human being?"* most people answer by saying, *"Give to them."* Some say, *"Give them love."* Typically, I need to ask the question several times before someone gets it.

QUESTION:

If it really is *"more blessed to give than to receive"*
what is the highest thing you can do for another human being?

ANSWER:

Allow them to GIVE to YOU.
Allow others to have that "Highest Blessing".

Let other people have the highest blessing. It does not mean to take from them. It means to simply allow them to give to you.

When your 5-year old offers to make your bed, let her do so to the best of her ability. Then, praise her for helping. Even if it is done all wrong, do not belittle her or even correct her. Take pictures of your "imperfectly" made bed and stick them on the refrigerator. Put a big note under the photo that says something like, *"Kelly did this for me today."*

When we do not let others give to us, we take away the opportunity for them to receive the highest blessing. Perhaps you worry about what others might think of you, and that it may appear that you are too weak to handle a problem yourself. Maybe you just do not want to be a burden. Or, it just might be when you are too busy, and you simply decide to do something yourself because it would take longer just to tell someone else how to do it.

To become a love-based leader when challenged or threatened, you need to take a different approach. When you are hurting and someone asks if something is wrong ... tell them. When someone asks if they can help you with something, let them. Sharing with others and letting others give to you does not mean you are weak, unless you become a taker. If you do that, you will become your own worst enemy.

A love-based leader is never a taker. Additionally, a love-based leader is not only a giver, but an inspiration to get others to give at home, at work, at church, in the community, and even globally.

<u>The Man and The Wood Stove</u>

Imagine a man freezing in an old log cabin during a blizzard. Holding an armload of wood and standing before a cold wood-stove, he shouts, *"Stove, I'll give you wood just as soon as you give me heat."* Then he just stands there, freezing to death. Holding on to the one thing that will save him.

When you wait to give, until your boss gives you a promotion or your spouse gives you love, just as that man in the cabin, you freeze to death.

Quit focusing on what you are going to get. Instead, focus on what you have to give. Remember, a love-based leader creates great relationships by suspending judgment and giving value.

<u>Captain Dan and Laura</u>

In 1980, we were conducting our LifeStream Basic Seminar near Chicago. My father was the facilitator and I was the class coordinator. I expected a typical weekend of insights, breakthroughs, and commitments. What I got, however, was anything but typical.

Thursday evening began normally, with about 50 attendees introducing themselves and stating their objectives for the weekend. We knew something unique was occurring when Margaret introduced herself and her six children.

By itself, someone attending with their children was not unusual. Attending with six of them was definitely unique. The only family member missing was Margaret's husband, Dan, who was a captain in the Chicago Police Department. He wanted nothing to do with LifeStream.

Sixteen year-old Laura, the youngest, was the only one of the children who was not there by choice. Margaret made her to come to the seminar. She had even told Laura the classic line, *"This is for your own good."* This usually does not bode well, as classes like LifeStream are generally far more effective when participants choose to be there.

The first day must have seemed like hell for Laura. She resented being forced to come, and resisted any possibility of actually learning anything.

Nevertheless, little by little, Laura's resistance melted. By Friday evening, her exuberance, depth, and honesty had turned her into one of the leaders of the class.

Then, late Friday evening, there was a disturbance at the door. I investigated and encountered a uniformed Chicago police officer. Yes, this was her father ... Captain Dan.

Captain Dan demanded I take his family out of the class so he could take them home. From my previous experiences with Margaret, I knew he had a quick temper and that he was a heavy drinker. My fear-based reaction was to comply immediately (Facade), even though I wanted them to stay.

Captain Dan was an imposing presence. He was in his uniform, and he had his gun. It was not drawn, and there was no indication that it might be, but I could not have been more threatened if he had pointed it at me.

I grew up in Southern California. My only experiences with Chicago police were news reports of the 1968 Democratic convention riots. This man did not just intimidate me. He terrified me.

I have no sense of smell, and could not determine if he had been drinking. Since I knew he liked to drink, as far as I was concerned he was drunk. I was unprepared to deal with an angry and potentially intoxicated cop with a gun. I just wanted him to leave, and I would have immediately taken his family out of the class to accomplish this.

But, when I informed Margaret of the situation, she told me they would not leave. The kids all agreed. My father shared the problem with the rest of the class, who were all very supportive of this decision.

I felt this was a threatening and possibly dangerous response. As the messenger, I did not relish telling Captain Dan that his family was refusing to leave the seminar. I was not trained on how to handle a possibly drunk Chicago police captain with a gun, especially one perceiving me as holding his family hostage. I began to question my career choice.

Amazingly, there was a police captain from a different police department in that class. Captain Emil offered to tell Captain Dan that his family did not wish to leave the class. Unlike me, Captain Emil was trained on how to handle such situations. It was this ability, plus the peer pressure he exerted as a brother police captain, which enabled him to diffuse this conceivably dangerous scenario.

When Captain Emil returned to the room, he invited Margaret and her kids to be guests in his home for the remainder of the weekend. He felt in this way they could finish the seminar without having to deal with probable turmoil at home. They readily accepted.

Captain Dan had gone. Margaret and her children had a place to stay for the weekend. I was relieved until I looked at Laura.

Laura was sitting with her arms and legs tightly crossed, sobbing. She was practically in a fetal position. Her father had disrupted the seminar she was beginning to enjoy. I was quite worried for her.

"Laura," I asked. *"Are you OK?"* I will never forget her answer.

Laura looked at me and said, *"These people will never know what a beautiful man he is."* I was stunned and awed. With this attitude, I knew I could work with her.

"Please, help me get my father to take LifeStream," she continued. *"He needs this so much."*

I was trying to be sympathetic, but I honestly did not want him in class. I never wanted to see Captain Dan again, not ever. *"Laura,"* I responded, *"I don't think that's possible."* I did not want to get her hopes up. In my own fear-based way, I was trying to be helpful.

Laura looked up and replied, *"This class has taught me I can do anything I set my mind to accomplish. Don't you believe I can reach him?"*

Thinking it would be a good idea to validate what Laura had been learning, I did a quick reversal. I told her it would not be easy, but she could get her father to take LifeStream. Even though I personally did not want Captain Dan in class, I gave Laura my best shot at a plan to reach him.

"I'll do anything. What do I need to do?" She responded.

"First," I began, *"close your eyes and imagine your father in the LifeStream Basic Seminar.* See him talking with the other students, listening to the lectures, and participating in the class. See him demonstrating the beauty you know he has. Imagine how people are responding to him."

"Now, pretend the class is over," I continued. *"It is Sunday night. How would he be acting? See that beautiful man. See how people are looking at him. How would that make you feel?"*

Laura's eyes opened and swelled with tears of joy. She said it would be the most wonderful thing in the world. *"Good,"* I said, *"that is all you need to do. Create this visualization before you go to bed every night, and re-create the feeling you just experienced. Will you do that Laura? Will you do that every night?"*

"Yes," was all she said.

"That is the easy part," I continued. *"Here is the hard part. From now on, you are to pretend your visualizations from the night before are not your imagination, but rather a memory of a real event. I want you to begin treating your father as if he has already taken the class."*

"Essentially," I said, *"You are going to play a mind game with yourself. You will need to demonstrate the same feelings of relief, joy, honor, and gratitude that you know you will have when he actually completes the LifeStream class, but you will need to do it in advance."*

"One more thing," I told her. *"You are not to ask your father to take LifeStream. Your mother has already tried to get him to take the class for months, and it has not worked. You have to treat your father with love until he sees the need to take the class for his reasons, not yours. Can you do that?"*

"I will," she responded. After a short pause, Laura asked, *"How long will I have to do this?"*

"Until he does the class," I answered.

Laura thought about this for a few seconds. *"OK"*, was all she said.

**"Your life works in direct proportion
to the commitments you make and keep."**

James H. Quinn

I figured it was unlikely this girl would voluntarily imagine her father attending the class every night, much less re-create these deep feelings on a daily basis. I figured that Laura would try it for a few days, give up, and then I would be off the hook.

I was safe. I would not have to deal with having Captain Dan in class. I would also be able to tell Laura the only reason it did not work was because she quit. It was the perfect plan.

However, I was about to learn the impact of a love-based leader. Laura kept her commitment. Every night she re-created the feelings of her father in class. More importantly, she demonstrated love-based leadership on a daily basis. She was determined to be excited, focused, and accepting of her father regardless of his reactions.

It took Laura about two months, and Captain Dan actually took the LifeStream Basic Seminar. Everything she wanted happened. The people in his class were blown away. Her father really touched the other students. More importantly, a dysfunctional family began to treat each other with love.

It is virtually impossible to resist the love-based leadership of someone you care about.

If Laura had been less committed, she would have given up long before she reached her father. As a result of her unshakable commitment, Captain Dan and the other students in his class all benefited from Laura's love-based leadership. So did her mother, sisters, brother and thousands of my students who have heard about their story.

I also benefited from Laura's love-based leadership. Captain Dan and I became friends. He took me ice-sailing on Lake Geneva and treated me to a Chicago Bears football game. I took him to a USC vs. Notre Dame football game. We became quite close.

When Captain Dan retired from the police force a few years later, other than family, I was one of the only "civilians" invited to the party. This is not how I would have imagined our relationship when we first met. I finally knew what my father meant when he told me to *"look deeper"* when I made judgments of people I did not understand.

Captain Dan -- The Rest of The Story

I wanted to be sure I had gotten this story as close as possible to the original events, so I sent the first draft to Captain Dan's oldest daughter, Danielle. She sent the following email, which provided me with deeper insights into the man who, at my first encounter, I thought was drunk and willing to use deadly force.

Dear Ross,

As you know my dad was a pretty amazing guy. Laura and I have always tended to think of our father as a beautiful man for very different reasons. I focused on his "strength." Laura, on the other hand, was the only sibling to engender "kinder" behaviors from him.

While intimidation is a consciousness I never had to contemplate, it was an attitude with which my dad was expert. He fostered it. My father knew if he wanted to be good at what he did, and in order to not have to be violent, he had to develop it.

As a direct result, my father became the youngest sergeant in Chicago history. In fact, dad was leading men during riots when he was only 25 years old.

It is not surprising he intimidated you at your first meeting. But I feel you had very little to worry about. He had that gun out of its holster I think only twice in his entire career, and I only know of one time that he brandished it at someone. My dad thought of the "gun" as part of the tools of his trade, not as a weapon. It was certainly not something to be taken out in a situation like LifeStream.

Even while being a challenging father, my dad was doing things in the world that probably saved many lives. He was in every major riot in Chicago from 1960 to 1985. Not one of his people was indicted following the Democratic Convention. This is because he was with them and, unlike many other senior officers, he told them what they could and could not do.

One of my early memories was when Dailey Sr. gave the "shoot to kill"
order for looters. My dad was on the street that night, and a young man was running down the street with a television on his shoulder. My dad took out his gun, and then said to himself *"I'll be damned if I am going to shoot someone over a television set,"* and put his gun away. At that instant, a bullet missed his head by about 6 inches.

When my father explained "why" he did what he did, I understood that the core of his understanding was that he was empowered by the people as a peace officer. That was his guiding principle.

My father understood civil liberty better than anyone I have ever met. He took his authority from the law and from the people who paid his salary. There are not many who naturally foster the level of intestinal fortitude my dad did. I see a combination of a mental fearlessness and a personal commitment to "my word, that which I speak into the world."

Having that sort of personal integrity has always been amazing to me and I don't encounter it often, still. I firmly believe my father lived as long as he did, because he did your training. I know for sure it is the reason that he had "any" relationship with his children during the years preceding his passing. We wouldn't have been able to "get over" our history as well, without LifeStream.

While we have had our struggles and more, people have constantly commented on how close my family is. We cooperate in a way I think many families never do, and truly approach each other with deep respect.

Not a week goes by that I don't consciously use something that I learned from participating in your seminars. Now, 28 years later, it is still the most profound experience of my life.

Love and Light Always,
Danielle

The Widow

John and Mary lived the kind of relationship few of us have realized. They were in college when they first met. It was not a "love-at-first-sight" fairy tale. In fact, Mary's first impression of John was that he was obnoxious. John thought Mary was attractive, but stuck-up.

Because theirs was a small college, it was not uncommon for them to bump into each other. They were always cordial, but certainly not overly friendly with each other.

However, Mary's younger sister, Nancy, thought they would make a great couple. Nancy tried to arrange meetings between them. She was unsuccessful at several attempts, but finally struck gold.

Nancy bought two tickets to a Chicago Cubs game, and asked John if he would like to go. John was not particularly interested in Nancy, but being a Cubs fan he naturally accepted the invitation.

Nancy knew that her sister was a rabid Cubs fan. On the day of the game Nancy pretended to be sick and asked Mary to take her place at the game. Mary actually accused her sister of faking in order to finally get her and John on a date. It took several sickly denials but Mary relented and accepted the ticket. After all, she thought, *"Everybody is a little obnoxious at a baseball game. How bad could it be to go with John?"* Actually, pretty bad.

John refused to pay for a high priced parking spot near Wrigley Field, and by the time he finally found a spot the game was underway. The long walk meant that it was well into the second inning before they found their seats.

Mary was not happy. She was irritated that they had missed seeing the Cubs score in the bottom of the first inning. The situation did not improve when the Dodgers scored in each of the next few innings to take a commanding lead.

Trying to set things right, John went to get some hotdogs and beer. On his way up the stairs with the food, some kids bumped into John, causing him to spill everything all over himself.

Standing a couple of feet away from Mary, he ran his finger through the mustard and beer covering his shirt and put it in his mouth. Looking directly at her, John smiled and said, *"It's delicious. Want a taste?"*

That is when it began. Mary thought John would explode with anger when the food was flung all over his clothing. Instead, she saw a confident humor that really stated, *"This is no big deal. I might as well have some fun."*

In short, John melted Mary's icy barrier and she burst out laughing. After that, John and Mary had a ball. They began by sharing their favorite Cubs stories, and ended up the day agreeing to go out on a real date. Two years later, they were married.

Over the years, John and Mary experienced all of the events that can adversely affect marriages: children, job problems, money problems, religious differences, and parental interference. But each challenge only served to make them closer and more supportive of each other.

They rarely disagreed and never fought. Even though Mary tended towards the appropriate side, John's antics only brought her joy. Then the unthinkable happened.

Not long after their 46th anniversary, a drunk driver killed John. Somehow, with the help of her family, Mary managed to move her body through the ritual of John's funeral.

All most people could do when they approached her was to hug and say, *"I'm so sorry Mary. If you need anything, anything at all, please just call."*

Mary would politely say, *"Thank you, I will. Thanks for coming."*

As I watched these exchanges, a thought came over me. The statement, *"If you need anything, please just call,"* has to be one of the safest offers of all time. The one thing most people in a similar situation are almost certain not to do, is call.

Over the next few weeks, people dropped by her house with casseroles and gifts. Little by little the attention waned, and Mary went into a world of survival and coping. But, her light slowly went out. Coping was not "living".

It was Nancy who saw that something had to be done. She tried taking her sister out to dinner, and inviting her over to play cards. Nothing worked. Finally, she got an idea.

A few weeks after the funeral, she made Mary a nice meal and took it to her home. Upon arrival Nancy said, *"Hi Hon, I just brought you a little something to freeze for a day when you don't want to cook."*

Then, in the kitchen as they made room for it in the freezer Nancy asked her sister, *"Could you do me a big favor? My church is having a bake sale and it would be a huge help if you could make a couple of dozen cookies for me to sell."*

Mary was still overwhelmed with grief and was withdrawing from life. There was not a chance she would ever ask for help of any kind. However, the one thing she could not do was to refuse the request of someone else who needed her help, especially her sister. She said yes.

"Givers Gain, and Takers Lose"

Unknown

This was the new beginning for Mary. After baking the cookies, and getting out of the house to deliver them to Nancy's church, she started visiting friends, going to movies, and even joined her sister's church. Soon, she was one of its most reliable volunteers. She never stopped grieving her loss of John, but she stopped letting the grief imprison her.

It is more blessed to give than to receive. Nancy's leadership created the space for Mary to experience some blessings at this traumatic time in her life, by choosing to give. The alternative of falling into a deep Freeze reaction never really took hold.

Love-based leadership really breaks down to just two things. Choose to be a giver, and inspire others to become givers.

Your Urges and Reasons to React,

Cancel Your Ability to Give

EXERCISE #4 - Choosing To Give

1) Describe a time when another person gave to you, even though you had hurt their feelings. Perhaps a friend helped you to change apartments, even though you had forgotten his or her birthday.

_____

_____

_____

_____

_____

2) Describe a time when you gave to another person, even though they had hurt your feelings. Perhaps a partner was critical of you, and then needed a favor. Instead of withholding because of your resentment for being hurt, you instead chose to let it go and help him or her out.

_____

_____

_____

_____

_____

3) Describe a current negative circumstance that is causing you to feel resentment for, and to withhold your gifts from, a person you care about. Now game-plan a love-based strategy for giving your gifts to that person.
(Suggestion: Start small)

_____

_____

_____

_____

_____

91

The Love-Based Leader in Business

It has been calculated that 80% of the results in business
are created by only 20% of the people.

Successful **20th** Century *Position-Power Fear-Based Leaders* had
the ability to attract, train, develop, and retain those in the top 20%.

Successful **21st** Century *Love Based Leaders* will have the ability
to attract, train, develop, and retain those in the top 20% ...

who will then duplicate themselves by inspiring these people
to attract, train, develop, and retain those in the top 20% ...

who will then duplicate themselves by inspiring these people
to attract, train, develop, and retain those in the top 20% ...

etc ... etc ... etc ...

Traditional *Position-Power Fear-Based Leaders*
created *Fear-Based Followers*.

Successful 21st Century *Love-Based Leaders* will
create *Love-Based Leaders*.

CHAPTER 4

Love-Based Leadership?
In Business?

When I first introduced the concept of love-based leadership in a business seminar, one of the reactions was, *"Love-Based Leader? In business? There is no love in business!"* I was reminded of Tom Hanks in "A League of Their Own" when he said, *"Are you crying? There's no crying in baseball."* Nevertheless, many baseball players have cried during a game. Even tough guy Pete Rose cried on the field.

Just as there is crying in baseball, there is love in business. I always felt fortunate when I had a job that I loved. Whenever I was in a sales position, if I made a sale I really loved my new client. Any time I was promoted to a higher-paying job, I always loved it. Several of my clients, and many former co-workers, have become close friends with whom genuine love and affection continue.

I could go on. But Kahlil Gibran (The Prophet) describes the concept more eloquently. He said, *"My work is my love made visible."*

My mother was fortunate to have been able to spend time with Mother Teresa. While at lunch, she asked her, *"Mother, what does prayer mean to you?"* Interestingly, Mother Teresa's answer was somewhat similar to Gibran's:

> *"Prayer is work in action, and work in action is prayer."*
>
> Mother Teresa

Most people did not see Mother Teresa as a businesswoman. But do not doubt it for a second. She was the head of a global organization, The Sisters of Charity, which still depends solely on contributions inspired by Mother Teresa.

It is important to realize that when we truly love our work, we are giving love. You do not have to be Mother Teresa to give love in your vocation. You can heal and bring joy to others with a cup of coffee and a kind word, or by mending broken fences. Providing goods and services that others need to thrive or survive is in itself a form of love.

Much of the giving in the business world is Fear-Based:

"I'll work harder if I get a raise."

"If I don't prospect for new clients, I'll lose my job."

*"I'm not going to support her project,
because that will put her ahead of me for a promotion."*

*"He didn't help me when I was behind schedule,
so I'm not going to help him now."*

The business and educational segments of our society have done a remarkable job in the development and teaching of job skills, or task skills. As a result, huge numbers of people are generally competent at their jobs. Corporations are filled with people who know what to do and how to do it, yet job dissatisfaction and high rates of employee turnover are rampant.

Love-based leadership requires a higher standard, a change in thinking. The businesses that will succeed in the 21st Century will not have the luxury of depending on position-power fear-based personnel, who simply react negatively to problems such as low-productivity, off-shore competition, new government regulations, and office dramas.

The successful companies will be the ones that attract, train, develop, and retain quality personnel who are love-based leaders. These are the people who will create the profitability that will enable the company to attract an increasing stream of love-based leaders.

Fear-Based Reacting is a habit.
Love-Based Leadership can also become a habit.

Start small.
Build your competency as a Love-Based Leader.

Pro-Act

The alternative to reacting to a problem, or pre-acting to the possibility of a problem, is not necessarily easy to do. However, it is simple. You simply notice how you are reacting or pre-acting, and, then choose to do something different. Almost anything would be an improvement, but conscious decisions to implement a love-based solution will prove most effective. Later in the book, we will explore four positive alternatives to the four fear-based reactions.

Unfortunately, because we have been so thoroughly conditioned to be reactive, there is not even a word for the opposite of "react" in the dictionary. The closest you could find was "act", which implies a phony or artificial response. However, a word has been coined which does work. Instead of reacting, we can now choose to "Pro-Act".

> **To Pro-Act is to become a Professional at Living.**

Instead of a *"do as I say, not as I do"* approach, pro-acting is the demonstration of the alternatives you would choose to have others implement, regardless of negative circumstances or hurt feelings.

Because love-based leaders are pro-active, they tend to prevent and solve problems. At the very least, pro-active love-based responses will keep a difficult situation from escalating into something much worse.

Imagine a scenario in which you are attacked while walking down the street to catch a bus to work. You are punched violently and knocked to the ground. Your attacker then jumps on your chest and strikes your face while swearing at you and spitting. It is painful, insulting, and disgusting. You have never seen this person before, and have no clue as to why this is happening. How would you react?

Depending on the size of the threat, your abilities, and your training, you might fight back or run away. Otherwise, if you could not get away, you could yell for help and cover-up to reduce the damage. You might even try to talk the person into stopping by telling him what you think he wants to hear. Fight, Flight, Freeze, or Facade. Because you are angry, frantic, confused, or scared, you could employ one or more fear-based reactions to protect yourself.

Now imagine a second scenario. You are walking down the street and hear the squealing of brakes. You turn and observe a car striking a pedestrian. He literally flies through the air and lands at your feet. Blood is spurting from his arm, where a bone is protruding.

You become pro-active as you bend down to help the man, but in his delirium, he strikes you harder than the previous attack. This man is also swearing and spitting as he continues to hit you. It is as painful as the first example, but with more swearing and saliva. Blood is ruining your clothing.

With even more negativity than the previous circumstance, how would you react? Would you react the same way as the first example? If you bent down to help the person and were hit, would you stand up, kick them, and leave in anger? Of course not. You would remain pro-active.

You might wrap the wound in your good shirt, even while blocking the punches. If a drunk offered to help, you would keep him away. If an ambulance showed up you would turn the man over to them in a heartbeat. You would be determined, careful, and open for help. You would be an effective leader even while enduring pain, spit, fear, and insults. You would do so even if you had been depressed all morning.

There is only one difference between the two examples. In the second example, you could see "why" you were being hurt. Because of this you did not take the "attacks" personally, and you were able to maintain self-control.

When operating as a fear-based reactor, you are more concerned with your problems than with your destination, and your life then becomes the effect of your circumstances. Much as the automatic-pilot on an airplane, you only react to outside forces. Thinking is not required.

On the other hand, when operating as a love-based leader, you are more concerned with your destination than with your problems, and your life becomes the cause of your solutions ... in spite of your circumstances. A live pilot can make choices to fly above, around, or through turbulence to arrive safely at the desired destination. Thinking is required.

The Restaurant Manager

The following letter regards a serious business problem, and a solution. It is a true story of a breach of trust. Do not simply read the letter. Imagine yourself as each of these people, and ask yourself how you would have acted had you been in their place.

Read carefully, and read between the lines. You will see all four fear-based reactions. Yet it only took one love-based leader to inspire a love-based solution.

Dear Ross,

I want you to know that today you've made a difference in my brother's life, and he hasn't even met you. Here is what happened.

My brother owns a restaurant in Texas. Two weeks ago he discovered money was missing from a deposit. He suspected that it was taken by his long-time manager ... a valuable employee who knew the business inside and out.

He asked the manager if he had any idea what happened. The manager said, *"I won't lie to you. I took it. I planned to pay it right back, but it took longer than I thought. I'm sorry."*

My brother's policy on this stuff is clear. You fire the guy, no matter what. We spoke on the phone the day it happened. I suggested to my brother a revolutionary concept. Instead of making a fear-based decision, I challenged him to find a creative win-win solution. I gave him an alternative to firing this man, but I got off the phone thinking my words had fallen onto deaf ears.

Two hours later my brother called back. The man and his wife had come to my brother's office with a check from his parents for the entire sum.

During the ensuing discussion, his manager had told him that he took the money to pay for his daughter's doctor bill. He knew he was losing his job. He just wanted to make it right.

My brother told me that before I told him about acting out of love instead of fear, he would never have considered keeping this man on. It would not have mattered how loyal he'd been, or how compelling the circumstances.

To make a long story short, my brother did not fire him. He put the man on probation, and demoted him to a position where he won't handle money, but will be able to earn a living. My brother then gave him part of the money he'd taken as an advance on his salary (since he knew things were tight).

From what I know about this situation, and how my brother dealt with it, I believe he took a potentially tragic episode and turned it into a wonderful opportunity. This man might well become the most loyal, devoted employee my brother will ever know, just because someone was willing to take a chance on him.

For one moment my brother ran his company with wisdom and compassion, not fear. Even that one moment is a tremendous gift.

So Ross, here is how you made the difference. First, I didn't even know the words "Fear-Based" reacting until you taught them to me.

Second, I would never have suggested a love-based approach to anyone in my family (even if I knew it was the right thing), simply out of fear they would reject me. Because of that, my brother touched his manager.

That man has a job this Christmas because I had the courage to risk rejection for something important, and because my brother had the courage to think "outside the box." Who knows whom his manager will touch because of all of this?

As for me, I'm willing to keep risking for what I believe in. Thank you for showing me that I could make a difference.

Merry Christmas,
Love (name withheld by request)

The Win-Win Principle

Increasingly, successful organizations are defined by their effectiveness in aligning human resources with corporate objectives. The biggest business winners in the 21st Century will be corporations run by love-based leaders, who operate their companies in accordance with the "Win-Win" principle.

> **I cannot win, and sustain it ... unless you also win.**
>
> **You cannot win, and sustain it ... unless I also win.**

While this concept is well known, it seems poorly understood and often undervalued in the modern corporate culture. As an employer, you may think you are succeeding when you get more than you give to your employees.

If you are a smart employer, you have hired smart employees. Such people know when they are being taken advantage of. Ultimately, they will react to you. You will lose your best people. They will either quit or hold back. Either way, you and your company stand to lose out.

As an employee, you might feel you are getting away with something by leaning on another person or for getting paid for more than you are giving to your employer. At best, you will fail to achieve your potential. At worst, you could be overlooked for promotions or even fired.

By adhering to the "Win-Win" principle, love-based leaders rise to the top. As employees, these people give more than they expect in return. They arrive early and stay late. These people ask, *"What can I do to help take this company to the top?"*

These love-based leaders avoid vengeful or counter-productive behaviors, choosing instead to take actions that are aligned with the goals and objectives of the organization. They do so even when they feel threatened or even attacked by colleagues. Often, these leaders spend their own time studying the industry and the competition, and then freely share ideas that they feel will improve their company.

In sales, love-based leaders make sure their customers get what they want, when they want it, while providing service in every way possible ... and are continually looking for ways to provide added value. Commitments are completed earlier and better than expected, and the client always gets more than they paid for.

In management, love-based leaders take care of their employees. They do not play politics. They ethically reward and promote the effective employees who continually do the right thing for the organization. These managers give positive and non-judgmental feedback when their employees make a mistake.

Effective love-based managers know that their professional success depends on the success of every member of their team. Those who really desire to succeed will inspire their people to discover reasons to become love-based leaders.

If you are working for an organization that does not follow this principle, you are not helpless. You have the same 3 choices as "George" (Chapter 2) ...

1) Change the company from the inside.

2) Get a job with a company that recognizes and rewards value.

3) Start your own company.

In the workplace, because almost everyone has his or her own agenda, people's needs, desires, and personalities often conflict. It might be nice to think of having a magic wand you could wave over everyone to bring instant harmony and accord, but the reality is that there will occasionally be adversity in even the best of families and corporations.

Nevertheless, your fear-based reactive efforts to take responsibility for changing anyone else's negative, non-productive, or destructive behaviors will be just about as effective as their attempts would be to change yours. Resistance, resentment, and revenge are the only likely results.

People may be ignorant of their own shortcomings, but they are not stupid. They have their own reasons for their fear-based behaviors. They will not change them for your reasons.

No matter how justified they seem, *"eye-for-an-eye"* reactions, or *"bury your head in the sand"* solutions only set the stage for the Reactive Cycle, which cannot work in the long run. The only sustainable answer is to identify and overcome your own fear-based reactions by becoming a love-based leader.

The Business World Is Changing

The vast majority of the world's largest corporations in 1900 are no longer in business. The Fortune 500 list from just 20 years ago only slightly resembles today's list, and it is changing even as you read this chapter. Current and past achievements do not equate with future successes.

Over the last century, the premise in the business world has often reflected two basic principles:

1) The leaders of a company needed to have a clear vision and a strategic plan for its achievement.

2) Management's job was the successful implementation of that plan through the fear-based motivation, manipulation, and control of its employees and staff.

99

Nevertheless, despite the overwhelming emphasis on this old structure, fear-based management techniques are rapidly losing effectiveness. Globalization, the Internet, and increasing political, social, and competitive pressures are having a dramatic effect upon the business culture in America, and everywhere else.

Not only are an ever-increasing number of people not operating in alignment with corporate strategic plans, there is an increasing problem with staff turnover and employee dissatisfaction. As a result, more and more top-level people are leaving to work for competitors, or to start their own businesses.

The problem (and opportunity) is that the average employee has easy access to more knowledge and information than an entire corporation could obtain in the 1960's. Additionally, far more employees are trained to be much more creative than in the past. As a result, they often have their own agenda of what is needed for the company.

When this occurs, not only does it frustrate the employee, it can place the employee out of alignment with corporate strategy. This will reduce the effectiveness of even the best strategic plan.

With the business world changing so rapidly, what now determines an organization's ability to survive and thrive is management's ability to Pro-Act and create consensus with independent thinking employees, staff, vendors, and customers. Organizations which are run by people who are oblivious to this fact, are doomed.

Creating Consensus

Love-based leaders strive to create consensus in order to achieve results with others. They realize that their egos must be put aside, and they then operate with the premise that there is seldom a single solution to any problem. Unanimity is rarely achievable, and is not the goal of consensus.

Consensus is the result of both individual choice and teamwork.

CONSENSUS = AUTONOMY + UNITY

Consensus is that state of agreement where all members of the group can say with integrity:

"This is the best alternative the group will be able to agree on, that I can and will support, even if I personally think there is a better choice."

In my outdoor leadership seminars, I have noticed that groups often spent more time debating the best solution to a problem-solving game, than it would take to test every single one of the suggestions. Further, once a solution is found, those who saw their ideas tossed aside usually do not celebrate the final solution.

Fighting for your solution can cause others to resist your ideas and suggestions, and to resent you if their ideas are ignored. By endorsing other ideas before your own, effective alternatives are often found. Besides, it is usually better to have consensus on an "inferior" solution than resistance on a "perfect" one.

Typically, when we spend time debating the best approach to solving a problem there are winners and losers. The winners may or may not be arrogant about their victories, but the losers are invariably resistant and are often resentful. The love-based leader in business uses techniques for creating consensus as a roadmap for eliminating this resistance.

When there is consensus the people of the organization are in agreement, *"We have the best product, or president, or pricing,"* or *"We have to save our jobs,"* or *"We have to beat off-shore competition."* When the people of an organization are in consensus, their various tasks and activities automatically operate in alignment. This synergy is actually the by-product of consensus, and not a goal within itself.

For example, I have observed that almost every time management fails to change an undesired behavior of its employees, it turns out that there is a company policy or a management behavior which actually causes, and usually even rewards, this behavior. Consensus is the best way to discover the disruptive policy. This will lead to an effortless change in the undesired behaviors. It always works.

When effectively creating consensus, there is even a tendency for numerous small groups within an organization to come to identical solutions to problems … with one exception. If the president, owner, or manager is in a group, that group will typically reach a different conclusion.

The most likely reason is that many people loathe being rejected by a poor manager so they give input too carefully. Thus, ideas are lost. Conversely, in an effort to help excellent managers, people tend to filter their input in order to either make their boss's decisions easier, or to impress them. Again, ideas are lost. In both cases it is the position-power of the boss, real or assumed, which prevents the creation of true consensus.

Consequently, consensus requires the traditional boss/leader to be very clear that his/her voice is just one voice. It is generally best for them to hold off giving his/her ideas and opinions until group consensus is imminent.

Additionally, to assure an open dialog, the traditional boss/leader needs to refrain from endorsing or criticizing any of the ideas being presented during the problem-solving by consensus session. Perhaps even more importantly, it requires that all members of the group knows ahead of time, that the boss/leader will make every effort to implement the final consensus. Otherwise, there is no point to the exercise.

The Distributor

I consulted with the Canadian distributor of five different product lines, one of which was a luxurious line of stuffed animals. Most of its sales came from this one product line. Unfortunately, the suppliers of their other four product lines were threatening to change distributors due to their low sales volume from this distributor. This would represent a potential loss of 25% of their total sales revenue, and would mean the company would not be able to cover its fixed costs.

The president knew he had to do something, so he started using his position-power to demand increased sales from the other four product lines. He tried threats, contests, pleading, and bonuses. Nothing worked.

Starting with the assumption that there are reasons for all behaviors, I set out to discover what was motivating the sales force to focus only on one product, even when they knew they needed to sell the other four as well. The first thing that I discovered was a "Comfort Zone". By selling the stuffed animals, which required little effort, almost everyone on the sales force was making a good living.

The second thing I discovered was the contests, the boss's pleas, the bonuses, and the threats had little or no effect because of fear. Almost to a person, the sales force was worried about losing existing customers. They thought it might upset their customers to push products they had already refused. Additionally, they generally felt that prospective customers would only be interested in the stuffed animals, so they did not want to blow new sales by pushing the less desirable products.

This was interesting, but it did not give me what I was looking for. I sat down with the president to discuss my findings. He spoke to me of his desire for employees to be successful, and he reiterated his concern that they were not responding to his requests.

I discovered the company policy that had unintentionally set this up. The president told me he especially wanted new hires to be successful so efforts at training them would not be wasted. He encouraged his managers to help new hires create a customer base with the easier to sell stuffed animals.

I was impressed. This man was actively pursuing the win-win concept. The new hires would win by receiving commissions that exceeded their minimal training draw. The managers would win with higher bonuses tied to their total sales volume. The president would win by increasing sales and reducing the amount of time he had to pay a training draw.

My second step was to conduct a problem-solving session with the managers, sales-people, and the president. First we broke into small teams to solve a hypothetical problem. Everyone learned the basics of how to create answers by consensus.

Once they had the idea, I presented the boss's dilemma, *"How can we get the sales force to sell more of the four other products?"* Each team was to come up with a possible solution. The only ground rule was each team member had to be able to support the team's idea, even if they personally thought there was a better answer.

One by one, I read each team's very similar suggestions. The solution was obvious.

My recommendation to the president went as follows: *"New hires have traditionally been trained to sell the stuffed animals first. The consensus of your employees is that from now on, all new hires should ONLY be allowed to sell the other four product lines. Only when they reach a certain sales volume will they be allowed to sell the line of stuffed animals."* He agreed to implement the policy. As far as I could tell, he had nothing to lose.

A year later I was invited back to do a follow-up seminar. This is always a good sign. I asked about the results of the policy change on sales. The president smiled and told me, *"Sales of the four smaller product lines are up 50%, and the stuffed animals sales are up 20% as well. We are looking to add a few more product lines."*

I asked what he believed had happened. He explained that because his managers had to focus on the other four product lines while training new hires, everything changed. Not surprisingly, when the new hires became proficient at selling the other four products, they had little trouble selling the popular stuffed animals. Not bad, but the sales turn-around was really caused by something else.

The minute the managers changed their focus to training new hires to sell everything but the stuffed animals, virtually all sales-people began selling more of those other product lines as well. The people who resisted changing when the boss had demanded it, voluntarily changed right along with the implementation of the new training policy.

In this case, the president became a more effective leader when he began to realize his people did things for their reasons and not his. Instead of trying to use position-power to change his sales force, he changed himself by allowing for a policy to be set by consensus.

Guidelines for Creating Consensus

Making a decision which directly affects only yourself is difficult enough. Working together in a family, where individuals have different wants and needs, can be even more frustrating.

However, the creation of consensus within an organization can be overwhelming. This is because most businesses are still run by dictatorial, position-power fear-based management. Fortunately, when done properly, the creation of consensus is still possible in those companies.

Solving problems with consensus involves change. In order to overcome resistance to change, all participants must commit to keep the following agreements.

#1: Advance Agreement to a Final Decision

For large organizations, form discussion groups of from 5 to 8 people. For small companies and families, one group is ample. The members of each group need to agree in advance to support the final decision of the group, even if they disagree with that decision.

#2: Agreement of Equality of Opinion

All people must be prepared to share their position as logically as possible, but each person agrees to avoid arguing for their own solution. Conflicts need to be avoided, but be wary of quick agreements, which may mean that some ideas have been left unspoken. Always make sure everyone has shared at least one idea.

#3: Agreement to Seek Acceptable Alternatives

All members agree to seek out next-best acceptable alternatives when an impasse occurs, and that there will be no voting. Each person agrees to yield to positions that have some logic, and at least a possibility of success, even if individually they feel there is a better solution.

The Two Objectives of Consensus:

1) Group ALIGNMENT for the process of solving a problem.

2) Group CELEBRATION for each failure, not just for each success.

"Well Days" at the Warehouse

Here is an example that illustrates how the consensus process was used to easily and quickly solve a serious internal problem.

Another company's needs for an accurate and timely inventory traditionally caused great stress between Christmas and New Year's. This difficult task was compounded as many employees tended to call in sick during this period. Threats, directives, pep talks, and staff meetings all failed to correct this situation, which was destroying morale and productivity.

Near the end of a one-day seminar on consensus, I put this problem to the staff. First, they broke into small groups to solve a hypothetical problem. Then, each team was instructed to come to a consensus on what was causing this year-end rash of sick-days, and what their solution would be. As always, I insisted the president of the company be in one of the groups.

Virtually every consultation I have been involved with has had a similar conclusion, which held true to form for this company as well. All groups, except the president's, came up with the same reason for the problem, and the same solution. Even a good leader has trouble overcoming their position-power.

The Cause of the Problem:

Company policy stated "sick days do not accumulate". Since sick days are lost if not used in any one calendar year, people who had not used theirs felt they would be cheated of paid time off, simply because they had stayed healthy. They viewed sick days as a perk, and therefore called in sick at the end of the year. Indeed, many people had even gotten to the point of planning for this eventuality so they would have extra time to prepare for the holiday season.

The Solution by Consensus:

The company should change their policy to allow employees to use either paid "sick days" or "well days", neither of which would accumulate.

The Result:

People could call in "well" on a nice summer day, and not have to worry about getting caught. They could even show off their tans. Stress levels plummeted. Most people used up their "sick" or "well" days by the holidays. The few who chose to take well days at that time of the year were minimal. In fact, these people were not resented because everyone else knew they themselves had taken advantage of this policy during the year.

Whether they realize it or not, business and governmental
leaders typically make their decisions without all of the facts.

Consensus is the only effective alternative.

The larger the number of people involved in a decision,
the more perfect the answer becomes,
with a resulting increased alignment of actions.

EXERCISE #5 - Creating Consensus

Take a current situation at home or at work. Organize a group session to create a consensus solution. Test the idea and then journal what happened.

Most people strive to make a difference IN their life.

Love-Based Leaders strive to make a difference WITH their life.

CHAPTER 5

Our One Quest is Peace

I n the previous chapters, we have covered how to identify and overcome fear-based reactions, build trust, create consensus, and more. Everything presented has one thing in common with everything else: Eventually, the successful understanding and implementation of these concepts will always result in feelings of peace.

Internal, Interpersonal, and International

Our One Quest is Peace.

The quest for peace is universal. Usually we seek an "internal" peace associated with physical wellness and self-worth. Often the quest is for "interpersonal" peace, created from having fulfilling personal and business relationships. There is also a great longing for "international" peace, which comes from living in a predictable world where mutual respect exists between nations.

Throughout history peace, however temporary, has generally been achieved at the expense of someone else. We have fought for food, for land, for honor, for money, and for power. In a pre-1976, fear-based, win-lose, you-or-me world, peace was never available to everyone. Fear-based living at least provided a chance for temporary peace for some.

However, in a post-1976, love-based, win-win, you-and-me world, peace is now available to everyone. As such, fear-based living only limits the chance for peace. It is only by overcoming fear-based reactions, and living as a love-based leader, that you significantly increase everyone's chances for peace … personally, professionally, and globally.

109

The Dachau Survivor

In 1982, I attended a lecture in Evanston, Illinois. The events of that evening had a profound impact on my view of the power of forgiveness.

The speaker was relatively famous for his forgiveness messages, so most of the people in attendance were already supportive of this topic. It promised to be an inspirational evening for people who were, at least conceptually, quite open to his ideas. This was not a hostile crowd.

An impromptu survey of several people revealed I was one of the few in the audience who had not read any of the speaker's books. To remedy this situation, I went to the lobby and bought one. I thought I might be able to get it autographed.

The speaker came out to a rousing ovation, and spoke on the power of love and forgiveness for more than an hour.

He had us in tears one moment, then laughing a few minutes later. He spoke beautifully and effortlessly. Everyone was having a marvelous time.

Firmly he stated messages such as, *"You have to forgive your enemies. You have to forgive family members who've hurt you. Forgiveness is the key to peace and happiness."* People were practically cheering. So far, so good.

"You have to forgive strangers who've stepped on your toes, or even accosted you," he continued to even more applause. *"And you must forgive yourself for the people you've hurt."* We loved that one.

The speaker was on a roll. We responded with continued applause and cheering until he said something rarely heard in a public address.

He said,

"In fact, the Jews will never be free until they forgive Hitler."

Our celebration hit a wall, and there was an abrupt silence. You could hear a collective gasp of disbelief at what had just been spoken, followed by an explosion of vehemence, the likes of which I have never witnessed.

Almost as he said, *"In fact, the Jews will never be free until they forgive Hitler,"* a tiny woman in the third or fourth row stood up and started screaming at him. Her tirade was a mixture of profanity, insults, and tears. It was quite difficult to decipher, but what I could understand sent a chill down my spine.

It became apparent that she was a survivor of the Dachau concentration camp. It was clear her hatred for Nazis would not tolerate any attempt to diminish her resentment and loathing.

She lived in nearby Skokie. Many survivors of concentration camps settled in this community after World War II. There were probably several other Holocaust survivors in the audience, and many of their children. This was not the place to say, *"In fact, the Jews will never be free until they forgive Hitler."*

For several minutes, she spat her hatred at the speaker, and then literally collapsed from exhaustion into the arms of the people sitting next to her. For a moment it appeared she had actually died. Fortunately she had not, but she was totally spent.

I had been watching the speaker during her attack. Never had I seen a man so naked. He just stood there and took it. You could see the depth of compassion on his face. I watched him struggle to find something, anything, to say to her.

I wager that he wanted to come down off the stage, embrace her, and tell her he was sorry for what he said. Nevertheless, he knew the truth. Her hatred of Nazis was killing her.

He knew this woman really needed to forgive the Nazis, for her own sake. However, any response on his part, *"Hating the Nazis is killing you,"* or *"Forgiveness is divine,"* would sound like empty platitudes, and he knew it. He really had nowhere to go.

Then, I heard someone crying. This was the only sound in the theatre of stunned observers, and it began to attract attention.

A young man was standing and weeping. I wondered about what he might do. Finally, he spoke through his tears … with a thick German accent. If I live to be a thousand, I hope I never forget what he said that evening.

He began softly and with compassion. *"Ma'am. Nobody has a right to hate more than you do. I can't imagine the horrors you've lived through. I can't imagine how anyone could treat another human in the ways you and others were treated. What makes it worse for me, however, is you are literally speaking of my parents and grandparents. It shames me as a German. Nobody has a right to hate more than you do."*

"But," and he pointed at the speaker and continued quite firmly, *"you must listen to this man. I have been having the Holocaust shoved down my throat since I was a child. I have been made to feel guilty and responsible. It has made me angry because I was not alive when those atrocities occurred."*

"And I am not alone," he continued. *"Thousands, perhaps millions of other young Germans are fed up with being judged for acts that were committed by others. If it keeps up, they will react. You did not deserve to be treated the way you were treated, and we have not deserved to be made to feel guilty for it. Keep on hating. Hitler would approve."*

With that, he made his way through the crowd toward the woman. When he reached her, they embraced. The speaker visibly sighed with relief.

I watched as people reached in to hug the people, who were hugging the people, who were hugging the two of them. I would have given anything to be a part of that hug, but I was too far away.

However, the speaker was being ignored. So I went up on stage, and had him autograph my copy of his book.

Finally, he got everyone to take their seats and spoke some beautiful words. He did a great job of bringing closure to what we had all witnessed. However, I knew it was the words of this young man I would always remember:

> *"Keep on hating. Hitler would approve."*

Forgiveness

Most people do not easily forgive when they have been hurt. Resentment makes it difficult. Hatred makes it almost impossible.

The Reason Most People Do Not Forgive:

"If I forgive you for what you did, it implies what you did was OK.
Since what you did was not OK, I will not forgive you."

To resist forgiving is to rationalize the withholding of your love, abilities, and gifts. When you fail to forgive, you may or may not hurt the other person, but you definitely damage yourself.

Behold the magnificent apple tree, which never says, *"I only give my apples to the deserving."* Regardless of the reason, an apple tree that stops bearing fruit (their gifts) is in the process of dying. Similarly, a human who stops giving love (or any of their gifts) is also dying. We die emotionally at first, but eventually the rest of the body follows.

Negative reactions triggered by your resentment are fear-based. It does not matter if your reasons are important or petty, real or perceived; to do so means you have made a decision to allow others to run your life because of fear. The fact that you can rationalize the behavior only proves you would not otherwise have acted in such a manner. In other words, when you react to your fears, the negative circumstance is in control ... not you.

Forgiveness does not mean you condone the hurtful actions of another person. It does mean that you have decided that those actions are not going to control you. Choosing to forgive when the conditions are hurtful, especially when you are tempted to react with hate, is true self-control.

When you forgive, you are "giving forth" love. Obviously, the person you are resenting benefits when you forgive, simply because you are not striving to hurt them back. More significantly, however, you benefit when you forgive. Clearly the person who hurt you did not create the forgiveness ... you created it. As such, to forgive another is to stay in charge of your self.

Love-based leaders overcome their own negativity in spite of their problems and circumstances. I call them **"Visionaries"**.

People who live fear-based react negatively because of their problems and circumstances. They are what I have come to call, **"Victimaries"**.

Instead of reacting to your hurt, the answer is to strive to find love-based solutions to your negative circumstances. Choosing to forgive when the conditions are hurtful, especially when you are tempted to react with hate and anger, is a sign of a love-based leader.

Hate begets hate. Hating the haters is not the answer, for you have already chosen to emulate them in your own way. Or, as I heard a comic-pianist jokingly proclaim in the late 1960's:

> *"I know there are people in this world who do not love their fellow human beings, and I hate people like that."*
>
> Tom Lehrer

Their Daughter Was Murdered

She was the kind of daughter parents dream of. She was talented, lovely, athletic, intelligent, joyful, and full of dreams for her life. Then one day, tragically, she was brutally murdered.

Her parents died more than a little bit that day. In an attempt to cope, they turned her bedroom into a shrine filled with photographs, trophies, newspaper articles, art projects, and other memorabilia. Unfortunately, this monument served only to intensify their grief.

Months passed, and the more they focused on their loss, the worse their grief became. But a few months later, the girl's mother had a startling insight.

She asked her husband, *"If we'd raised a son who could have done such a thing to another person, just imagine the pain we'd be going through."* Unbelievably, she and her husband went to the parents of their daughter's killer to help them deal with their own grief and shame.

The deceased girl's mother created a healing connection with people whom most of us would have resented, avoided, or even attacked. She even influenced her husband to participate.

Realizing they could not change their circumstance, and unwilling to forgive the man who killed their daughter, these people instead found peace by choosing to create a circumstance in which they could be loving and giving. What a powerful and beautiful legacy for their daughter.

You may not agree with their decision. But you have to agree that it took courage.

We may have no control over our circumstances. But we do have control over ourselves and how we handle those circumstances. By their nature, love-based leaders do not follow the crowd. They find a course of action that works, regardless of what most people would do. Some people would call that the mark of greatness.

COURAGE

There is no trick to demonstrating love-based leadership when life is working. The challenge is to possess these leadership qualities when something, or everything, goes wrong. Whether you are threatened with losing something you want, or with getting something you do not want, courage is the one characteristic you will need to be able to control yourself, as opposed to losing control or trying to control those around you.

> *"What've they got that I ain't got?"* asked the Cowardly Lion.
>
> *"Courage!"* replied Dorothy, the Scarecrow and the Tin Man.

Yes, it can be challenging to identify and overcome our own fear-based reactions to any negative circumstance. However, to inspire others to do likewise is the true test of leadership. Your ability to discover and implement solutions requiring consensus will be in direct proportion to your willingness to be courageous. Courage, however, is not the lack of fear. Courage is an act in the face of fear.

When people observe others achieving personal and professional success, seemingly without fear, they often reach an erroneous conclusion. They think fear itself is the problem. Therefore, they decide, it will be by eliminating their fears that they will be similarly successful.

Effective leaders are sensitive to their fears. They are neither overwhelmed by their fears, nor are they in denial of them. Because of this, sometimes they are able to make conscious decisions to risk, in spite of their fears. At other times they choose to be cautious, because of their fears.

While we seek out feelings of joy and happiness in our quest for success, it is fear that may actually be the most valuable feeling of all. Fear of being hurt can keep us alive when there is danger. Fear of loss can warn us when we should not trust someone. Fear of dying can give our lives a sense of urgency.

Rock climbing, for example, begins with the assumption that something could go wrong. The high levels of fear of the real risk of falling become only perceptions of risk with the proper use of safety equipment. It is not courageous to face danger without proper planning and clear agreements. It is foolhardy.

My daughter Kelcey once overcame her fears to climb a 50-foot rock face. Her courage to overcome her fear of falling was inspirational. This experience was made possible because of quality safety equipment and expert supervision. Several times she fell, screamed, laughed about it, and continued climbing.

However, after completing her climb and unhooking her equipment, Kelcey jumped for joy off a small boulder and sprained her ankle. Because of her lack of fear, she perceived no need to plan for something going wrong. As a result, jumping off a little rock nearly caused a broken leg.

With jobs and relationships, just as with rock climbing, begin with the

114

assumption things might go wrong. The acts of pre-planning and making clear agreements are the career and relationship equivalents of having a certified climbing harness and properly manned belay ropes.

Rejection in business is always a possibility when you strive for consensus, ask for a sale, interview for a job, or make a presentation. Nevertheless, there is no more danger from rejection, than there is from falling while attached to a safety rope. You may not enjoy the feelings of rejection, but you are no worse off than before. Shake it off, learn from the experience, and do it differently the next time.

If you were to conduct a study of all effective leaders, you would find many differences. However, at their core you would discover one common characteristic ... courage. This element consistently separates the successful from the unsuccessful, and the great from the average.

Without fear, no act is courageous. Fear is required.

Courage is a victory over fear. Courage empowers you to overcome fear-based behaviors such as insecurity, anger, anxiety, procrastination, worry, indifference, obsession, and denial; which otherwise could sabotage your personal and professional results.

Whenever you have a fear-based reaction to negativity, you give your personal power away. Until you stop giving your power away, you will always find a way to fail. The cure for this "disease" of negativity is courage. When you develop the courage to do those things you fear, you become the master of your own life.

The single greatest reason people fail to succeed is the destruction of their personal power. Regardless of whether your self-worth was destroyed as a child, or your self-esteem has been trashed as an adult, your personal power can be restored with courage. The only moment that matters is now.

Having Fear is Not the Problem.
Eliminating Fear is Not the Solution.

Daniel

In 2004, I was invited to Panama to give a keynote address at a three-day business conference. While I had been conducting seminars for years, this was to be my first 1-hour talk. I was excited, but quite nervous.

Appropriately, my talk was entitled, "Get Over Yourself". I spoke about believing in your dreams, and then exceeding them. At the conclusion of my presentation I asked the question, "If only one person gets it, really gets it, then my talk today has been worth it. Are you the one? Are you the one who is going to achieve more than you have ever dreamed?"

During the evening, several participants approached me to thank me for the presentation and to confidently pronounce, *"I am the one."* Daniel was one of them, but with him there was something different in his tone. His was neither a wish nor a commitment. It was a simple statement of fact, and it touched me deeply.

Something else was different. Daniel was the only one in a wheelchair. His very pregnant wife was pushing him. I thought, *"Not on my watch."* I immediately took over that duty from her.

That was the beginning of my friendship with Daniel. Over the next three days, I came to find out that he had been injured in a training exercise while in the military. After several years of treatment the prognosis was that Daniel would never walk again, and his therapy was discontinued.

The conference ended, but Daniel and I stayed connected. Six months later, Daniel was able to do something that his military therapists had said would never happen. He was able to get around on crutches. He credited this miracle to what he had learned from me. I was a bit more than moved, but quite certain this was mostly due to his extraordinary attitude.

Then, about a year later, Daniel showed up to see me speak in the Bahamas without crutches! Not only that, but when I was too tired to take my wife dancing, he filled in for me.

Since then, Daniel has had many victories including going back to school and taking up Karate. Rather than try to tell you about them, I will let Daniel tell you in his own words.

116

Dear Ross,

The lessons you teach have transformed my life. As you know, I was consigned to a wheelchair or crutches for life. I had let my military injury win, crush me, and make me believe that walking again was impossible. I believed I was trapped via my circumstances to live in misery and pain.

I cannot stop thinking about how you about broke your back pushing my wheelchair up that ungodly hill in Panama. I can still see the beads of sweat raining off your brow and the redness of your face. At first, I felt so helpless and guilty that it was so difficult for you, but you showed me that you don't just preach love-based leadership, you live it.

When you said, *"Circumstances can NEVER be who you are,"* something pierced my soul like electricity and penetrated through my barriers of self-pity, hate, frustration, and pain. It was then I realized my happiness was entirely my responsibility, and NO disability has the power to take it away.

Until I forgave the military, I was consigned to a wheelchair for life. Today, I walk. I am (because I want to take my physical strength to the next level) now enrolled in a Kenpo Karate class. Although there are times where my hip does not want to cooperate I am finding greater strength and balance.

I am excited that at the end of the semester I will be testing for my yellow belt in Karate. I love it so much that I will continue on till I get my black belt (which will be a 2-3 year commitment).

I am taking two English writing classes, and last semester I was awarded 2nd Best Poet of the University. I have been receiving praise from peers, faculty and readers.

I am also taking three music classes where I am learning voice, composition and theory. I have multiple songs that I have written and will be going to a recording studio this year to get them on an album.

Today, I am Happy. Today, I am in Karate. Today, I am a Fighter. Today, I fight for my life because I deserve to live.

I thank God that you were the messenger I needed. I am forever grateful. You taught me, to believe in me. Thank you. Thank you. Thank you.

It all started with forgiveness. I am forever a believer in the impossible.

Daniel Lawrence Sabin

The Mirror Concept

I have often used Mother Teresa as an example of a love-based leader. People admire many different facets of her persona. For some it is her faith. For others it is her love for, and commitment to, *"the poorest of the poor."* By studying Mother Teresa, many have learned to emulate and demonstrate these qualities.

The MIRROR Concept:
That which you admire in others,
is a reflection of your own special gifts.

But if your definition of a love-based leader is limited to saints such as Mother Teresa, you will have put her on a pedestal. To say something such as, *"She is incredible. But I could never do what she does,"* is to diminish your own self-worth, which is a necessary quality of a love-based leader. You also belittle the actual effort of the honored person, who always had to overcome his or her own challenges and self-doubts.

It is ironic that the very act of praising a great person should have a limiting effect on the person giving the acknowledgement. When someone is in awe of, or even worships, a love-based leader they may engage in philosophical discussions about the person's qualities or accomplishments. However, because most believe they cannot reach the same level of accomplishment, they do not even take the first step towards becoming a love-based leader themselves.

"When you put someone on a pedestal,
you are really putting yourself into a hole."

Jan Sanders (my mother)

That does not mean you should not emulate the people you admire. On the contrary, if you truly want to discover your gifts and talents, seek to develop from within yourself that which you admire in another.

The Mirror Concept operates under the premise that it is not possible to recognize a great quality in someone else, unless you yourself possess elements of that same quality. Basically, if you see it, you got it.

Additionally, since no two people see exactly the same qualities in any other person, the unique qualities you admire in another are mirrors of your own unique qualities. It goes under the, *"It takes one to know one"* principle.

Martin Luther King Jr. is an excellent person to use with the mirror concept.

Some people admired his determination. For others it was his compassion. Many saw Dr. King's speaking ability as his greatest attribute, and others thought it was his commitment to non-violent protest. Just select one of his characteristics that you admire, and then strive to develop it in yourself.

Unfortunately, old habits die hard. To develop as a love-based leader, it is important to not set the bar too high. Start small and celebrate little victories. Then tackle bigger challenges.

Benjamin Franklin changed a habit every 21 days. Maxwell Maltz, in his book Psycho-cybernetics, determined that it takes 21 days to change a habit or belief. Attending a weekend seminar, or reading a book can only cause temporary effects, unless you practice and demonstrate the tools and concepts you learn for at least 21 days.

LIVING Fear-Based or LEADING Love-Based

I did not begin this work by teaching love-based leadership. My focus was on teaching people to create solutions to their personal and professional problems, by identifying and overcoming their own negative fear-based reactions. It worked very nicely.

Over the years, however, I realized something else was happening. Every time someone overcame their own fear-based reactions, their efforts always inspired others. Always.

The Best Definition of a Love-Based Leader:
Someone Who Inspires Others

That is not to say that they always reached the intended person or persons in the way they necessarily envisioned ... they did not. Nevertheless it became apparent that even failed efforts to overcome fear-based reactions had a positive effect on someone.

Yes, there was often a positive effect on the intended person. But sometimes the impact was on someone who was so impressed with the effort that they began challenging their own thinking. For example, after an unsuccessful attempt to reach a boss, someone else would say something such as, *"I can't believe you stood up to him without anger. I would have ripped his head off. How did you do that?"*

It was then that I realized that I had not been teaching people to choose between living fear-based or living love-based. I had been teaching them to choose between living fear-based or LEADING love-based. They did not need to strive to be leaders, it just happened.

Further observations revealed this leadership to be the automatic result overcoming any fear-based reaction, large or small. People did not need to take huge steps to become a love-based leader. Even small steps had impact.

Love-based leadership does not need to be a grand, complicated change in lifestyle or intention. It can be as small as wiping off the top of a messy ketchup bottle, instead of complaining to the waitress. By looking for small fear-based reactions to overcome, you will slowly but surely build your abilities as a love-based leader.

Instead of sharing your irritation about how long you waited to pay a toll, when you get to the booth tell the operator that you want to pay the toll for the car behind you. Sometimes, rather than grumbling about your rotten work environment, you might try giving someone a flower.

Two Flowers

When I challenge my students overcome their fear based reactions, and to create love-based solutions at work, there is usually some resistance. Many times people simply lack an idea they can get enthusiastic about. True, some people fear rejection, but even that is often just an excuse for not trying something new.

The solution is to start small and develop competency before you tackle bigger projects.

> *"It's not about doing great things.*
> *It's about doing small things with greatness."*
>
> Mother Teresa

The best ideas are usually simple. They stand out with their elegance. If you are stuck for an idea, the solution is to form a small master-mind group to come to consensus on one. I often split a seminar into a few master-mind groups to come up with creative solutions to each other's problems.

In one such group, a participant shared that he disliked how personal relationships tended to stay within each department in his company. He felt that each department had become its own little island unto itself.

Even though everyone in his company ate in the same lunchroom, most people tended to sit with the people from their department. Purchasing, accounting, computer processing, customer service, and every other department tended to eat in their own little groups. Even the sales department, when they were not having lunch with clients, tended to eat only with other people from the sales department.

His master-mind group came to consensus with an idea to change this. At first he laughed, but after some encouragement from his group, he decided to do it.

That night he bought two flowers on his way home. In the morning, he got to work early and placed one flower on the desk of someone in Quality Control, and one flower on someone's desk in Accounting. The next day he placed one flower on the desk of the Vice-President's secretary, and one in a work-station in Computer Processing.

This process continued for days. He would arrive early and place a flower on a different desk in two different departments. By the end of the first week, both people who received a flower were actively trying to find out who got the other one.

By the end of the second week, everyone was arriving in the lunchroom in anticipation of discovering which two people got flowers that day. Lunchtime became a joyous time of mingling and laughter.

Once, to avert suspicion, he even put a flower on his own desk. This continued for about a month, and he was never identified.

After he quit bringing flowers, he noticed that people continued to look for the recipients of that day's flowers. People were starting to miss the event.

Not long afterwards, he got to work to find that several people had purchased a flower for everybody. They had bought dozens of flowers and placed one on every desk, work-station, locker, and truck. People were more excited than when bonuses were handed out.

Lunch was never the same again. People are still trying to figure out who the "flower-person" was. Every now and then, he comes early and drops off another two flowers. Periodically, so do others. On more than one occasion, he has come to work to find a flower on his own desk.

He will never talk. He is having too much fun. So is everyone else.

"Man is the center of a circle, the circumference of which is determined by self-imposed limitations."

Mahatma Gandhi

Are people fighting to get into your life, or are they fighting to get out of it? Are you moving one step closer to global impact every day, or one step closer to solitary confinement?

> *"Everyone thinks of changing the world,*
> *but no one thinks of changing himself."*
>
> Leo Nikolayevich Tolstoy

The Penalty of Leadership

There is a penalty for choosing to live fear-based. Your dreams die a little bit with each fear-based reaction or pre-action. As a result, most people kill their own dreams long before their life is over. When they do get to the end of such a life, they have disappointments, regrets, resentment, guilt, shame, and blame. These are the people who did not achieve their true potential. Is this your destiny?

Merely discussing and philosophizing what you have read in this book, or elsewhere, will be a waste of time. You must take action if you want your life to change. In the words of my father, *"Given the opportunity, most people are prone to procrastinate."*

Possibly the greatest of all personal tragedies is to end your life with the thought, *"If only I had another chance."* Based on the number of chances most people waste, another life would make little difference.

It has been said that your dreams give your life value.

But it is how you live that gives your dreams value.

There is also a penalty for choosing to overcome your fear-based reactions and become a love-based leader. If you are unaware of this penalty you will be surprised and threatened when it occurs, and it will occur. To be aware of this penalty is to be prepared for it.

The penalty for living a life of excellence as a love-based leader is that you will be criticized when you fail. You will also be criticized when you succeed. Just as many before you, you may be ridiculed for your great dreams or new ideas. Some people will misinterpret your good intentions, and will reject you.

Therefore, before you begin your quest to live your life as a love-based leader, you need to ask yourself a question, *"Can I handle some rejection?"*

If not, or if acceptance by others is your only goal, then do not strive to be a love-based leader. Your fear-based reactions will prevent it, because approval-seeking is a full-time job.

In a world full of people living fear-based lives, just how does one consciously choose to live a life as a love-based leader? Now we come to the most important part of this book ... how to do it.

Attempting to be a love-based leader without possessing the tools to make it happen is just an exercise in futility. Let's face it, old habits die hard.

The next four chapters are dedicated to teaching you how to shift from living fear-based to leading love-based by using the "Four E's of Excellence." I challenge you to create a great life, a life of excellence. How to get there will become clear, if you spend just a few minutes a day within these four chapters.

Four E's of Excellence

ETHICS - ENTHUSIASM - EVALUATION - EMPATHY

Present in all truly effective personal and professional relationships, these elements could also be defined as vision, joy, determination, and compassion. Regardless of the names we assign, self-control is needed to demonstrate them in the face of negative circumstances.

When you become aware of your negative *Fear-Based Reactions*, it becomes easier to see how you are attempting to control others with actual or implied *Position-Power*. With that awareness, you will be empowered to utilize the tools in this section to change your life and your results.

Instead of focusing on what others are doing wrong, learn to use *"Four E's of Excellence"* to take responsibility for yourself. Your impact will be greatly enhanced as you experience the power of living your life as a *Love-Based Leader.* It is worth the effort.

Excellence is the Art of Self-Control

E T H I C S
X
C
E N T H U S I A S M
L
L
E V A L U A T I O N
N
C
E M P A T H Y

PART III
THE METHOD

Four E's of Excellence

ETHICS

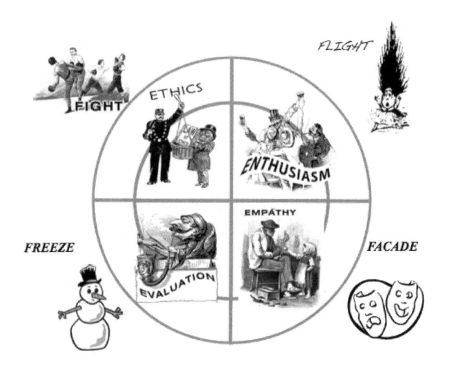

Results - NOT Excuses

"The result of most attempts at communication, is misunderstanding."

James H. Quinn

CHAPTER 6

ETHICS
The Alternative to FACADE

The FACADE fear-based reaction occurs when you take responsibility for the feelings of others. You try to protect them by saying what you feel they want to hear or what you think they can handle, instead of the truth.

The FACADE fear-based reaction also happens when you feel threatened or intimidated and try to protect yourself. Either way, whether it is to protect yourself or to protect others, you are trying to solve problems by clouding the facts, twisting the truth, or even lying. This rarely, if ever, ends well.

Regardless of your motivation, your Ethics are sacrificed when your comments are untrue: *"You look fine in that dress;"* or *"I'm sorry, it will never happen again;"* or *"I can change".* If you do not say what you mean often enough, eventually you will lose the trust of others.

When you demonstrate the FACADE fear-based reaction, you can easily end up hurt or angry when this causes you to be misunderstood or unappreciated. When you are worried, if your primary concern is to evade problems and conflict, your integrity will suffer ... often with disastrous results.

Ironically your FACADE fear-based reaction to prevent problems usually provides others with the justification of Fight, Flight, Freeze, or Facade reactions in return. FACADE fear-based reactions may delay, but do not prevent, the Reactive Cycle.

> *"Clarity at all costs ... or it costs you all."*
>
> Christine G. Quinn (my wife)

A typical FACADE fear-based reaction is to fake agreement to "keep the peace," which may have the opposite effect. Unless your intention is to have others react to you with negativity, you need to make a conscious choice to eliminate any perception that you could be lying.

Perhaps your intention is to be kind and supportive, but because you are "walking on eggshells", it can appear to others as if you are being insincere. If this behavior threatens them, and it often does, they will react to you. You, in turn, react to their reaction and the Reactive Cycle begins and escalates.

When you make a "boldfaced lie" intended to hurt someone, resentment invariably results. However, even a "white lie" designed to benefit another often creates problems.

Whether you remember it or not, you would not be using the FACADE fear-based reaction unless you had experienced being hurt when you tried to be honest. You might have been punished for being truthful. Maybe you shared a great idea, but were ridiculed by friends. Perhaps you were blunt and lost a friendship because you hurt someone's feelings.

Eventually, you developed the FACADE fear-based reaction as one of your defense systems. Perhaps feigning agreement kept people off your back. Pretending to love may have made you feel that you were being kind to someone you knew you were going to hurt with an eventual break-up. Coming up with convincing excuses may have protected you when something went wrong.

Whether you lie to protect someone else or yourself,
you may temporarily achieve desired results,
but the lie will eventually come home to haunt you.

FACADE fear-based reactions, as with all fear-based reactions, must have had some value (real or perceived) in order for you to have repeated them enough times to become habits. The good news is that once you realize they were chosen for value in the first place, you can choose to change the way you react for a higher value today.

Basically, to overcome FACADE fear-based reactions, you need to focus on what you want to CREATE instead of on what you are trying to PREVENT. This is especially important when doing so would seem likely to cause difficulties. Telling people what you think they want to hear, or what you think they can handle, often gives a short-term illusion of effectiveness. Eventually, however, this tends to create new problems.

If your relationship is important, strive to share your truth with kindness. Be direct in saying what you need or want, without filtering anything. It may help to remember that the FACADE fear-based reaction, even when motivated by good intentions, is still a lie.

"Sarge"

My father's mother, Lydia, had lived with us since I was a child. Her husband passed away from cancer shortly after my birth. Her strength and experience was a blessing to my parents.

My grandmother was a large woman, but her power was in her indomitable spirit. Everyone called her "Gram," not just family. However, my brother and I nicknamed her "Sarge" because she was so strong-willed. I have never met anyone with a greater love of people, or with less fear of rejection.

Sarge raised three successful sons ... Paul, James and Charles. In her lifetime she taught school, ran a ranch, managed a fabric store, was in charge of enrollments for our LifeStream seminars, and traveled extensively. At her passing, Gram's wake attracted hundreds of people. As a measure of her impact, almost half of those in attendance had never even met her.

When Gram was about 80, my mother began to notice she was emanating a body odor, even though her personal hygiene habits apparently had not changed. It kept getting worse and worse. Mom said nothing about it, as she did not want to hurt Gram's feelings.

> **Facade Fear-Based Reactions always involve a lie.**
> **Even the act of sparing someone's feelings**
> **can have terrible results.**

My mother casually started to question her. *"Have you changed your soap?"*, *"Have you started wearing a new perfume?"*, *"Are you using a new deodorant?"* Each time, Gram would respond that nothing had changed.

Finally, it got so bad my mother overcame her fears of hurting Gram's feelings and told her how offensive her odor was becoming. Gram was shocked, but not embarrassed. Nothing embarrassed her. Together they eliminated all possible causes of the odor, and decided to have it checked out by her doctor.

Testing confirmed cervical cancer. Surgery and treatment successfully took care of the problem. However, her doctor told them it could have been fatal had they waited much longer. It was very close. To this day, I remember my mother's lament; *"Gram almost died because I was worried about hurting her feelings."*

ETHICS

Ethics could be defined as the alignment of vision and behavior. The love-based leader behaves in a manner consistent with their ideals. He or she can develop trust, because promises are kept and results are achieved.

> **Consciously choose to make what you say will happen--happen.**

The ethical salesperson says, *"I will exceed my goals,"* and will do whatever it takes to do so morally and legally. He or she will overcome all obstacles. If it means calling on twice as many prospects to achieve a goal, then that is what will happen. If a family emergency comes up it will be handled. Afterwards, it is back to work with an even higher resolve. Intentions equal results.

However, many unsuccessful salespeople lack ethics. These people will set goals they do not believe in to pacify or to impress a boss or a spouse. By setting pie-in-the-sky goals, there will be two results:

They will fail because an obstacle, any obstacle, will beat them. This failure will NOT be their fault. They will have a good excuse, usually ending with a phrase such as, *"Besides, it wasn't really my goal anyway, it was my manager's."*

"Victim" stories are just excuses. Murphy's Law, *"If something can go wrong, it will go wrong,"* only provides uncommitted people with victim stories. True success results from honoring your commitments above reasons, justifications, explanations, and excuses.

At the core of ethics is honesty. Speak your truth, but do not kid yourself. People are your barometer. If people are reacting negatively to you, your idea of ethics is probably much like the proverbial "Bull in a China Shop". It is possible to be totally honest while demonstrating that you are doing so because you care. Your perceived Ethics will increase when they co-exist with love, calmness, gentleness, compassion, and respect.

It is important that you learn to speak the other person's language. If you are harsh with someone who needs understanding, you might as well be speaking Chinese to a German. They will not hear you.

Ethics begins with doing or sharing something worthwhile, and then by acknowledging the effort. It develops by noticing how others respond. If results are not forthcoming, change your approach. By learning to overcome your own fear-based reactions and then changing how you are expressing yourself (not just by getting louder), others will eventually get the point.

Remember, the FACADE reaction is fear-based. "White Lies" are justified in order to spare the feelings of others. Blatant lies can find their base in fears of poverty, rejection, abandonment, looking stupid, and so on. There is no limit to the rationale available for the FACADE fear-based reactions.

The love-based leader is not dependent on the approval of others. He or she knows when something worthwhile has been accomplished, even if everyone else decries or ignores the achievement. Decisions are made because they are in alignment with personal vision, not because they are popular. Whatever the "job" is, the focus is upon "getting the job done".

The following quote is often misunderstood, and is generally taken out of context:

"Winning isn't everything. Winning is the only thing."

Coach Vince Lombardi

However, Coach Lombardi's interpretation of "winning" changes the meaning of this famous statement. According to Bart Starr, his two-time Super Bowl champion quarterback, people rarely asked for Lombardi's definition of winning:

Lombardi's Definition of "Winning"

"Never go out to beat the other guy.
Only go out to be the best you can be. Then, you are winning."

Bart Starr (quoting Vince Lombardi)

The Problem: The FACADE Fear-Based Reaction

When demonstrating a FACADE fear-based reaction you strive to make things look better than they really are. Whether you are trying to protect yourself or someone else, you say what you think others can handle, or what you feel they want to hear. You are, or can appear to be, lacking integrity or lying.

You will ask yourself or others "Why?" types of questions:
"Why me?" ... "Why can't we just get along?"
"Nothing's wrong, why do you ask?"

When Negatively Consumed With FEELINGS & EMOTIONS,
Your Primary Characteristic Tends to Be WORRIED.

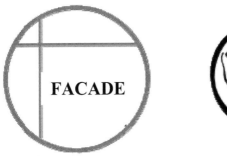 

I say one thing to your face, but I'm thinking something else.
Out loud, *"I'm fine. I'm just fine."* Inside, *"I'm hurt and angry."*
Out loud, *"I'll buy your product."* Inside, *"I'll cancel tomorrow."*

Other FACADE Characteristics:

**Intimidated   Defensive   Phony   Subordinate   Guarded
Guilty   Insecure   Inferior   Fragile   Needy**

The Extreme FACADE Fear-Based Reaction: DEPENDENT

Ask yourself,
"Do I usually feel responsible for other's feelings?"

132

The Solution: Add ETHICS

Be congruent by saying what you really mean. Tell people WHAT is happening, and/or WHAT you are going to do. You need to risk rejection, give others assurances, and let people know what you are truly thinking and feeling. Never let your negative, emotions, feelings, or issues get in the way of you creating "Desired Results".

> *"Never mind if people don't understand you,*
> *so long as no one misunderstands you."*
>
> R. Buckminster Fuller

Balance yourself with...

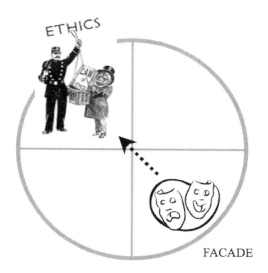

Choose to Become:

Accountable	**Thorough**	**Bold**	**Efficient**	**Decisive**
Determined	**Congruent**	**Focused**	**Honest**	**Confident**

Become "RESULTS" Oriented

The Tool: Creating Desired Results

Most people avoid setting goals. There is a simple reason for this. When people set a goal and fail, they feel defeated. The solution for many people, instead of learning from the experience, is to stop setting goals.

It is a little like the old joke, where a patient says, *"Doctor, it hurts when I do this,"* and he raises his arm over his head. The doctor then replies, *"Then don't do that."*

Instead of playing the old "goal-setting" game, we have changed the approach. If you are competent at setting and achieving goals, this should increase your effectiveness. If you have been struggling to achieve your goals, this system will change everything for you.

NO MORE "GOAL SETTING"
From now on use the terminology—Creating Desired Results

It may sound like semantics, and perhaps it is. Nevertheless, sometimes it is just a matter of changing your perspective a little in order to get your brain to cooperate. Open your mind and test out this technique. You will be amazed at the results you will be able to achieve.

Summary for Creating Desired Results

1. Important, Challenging, and Positive

2. Achievable

3. Specific, Measurable, Time-Sensitive Events

4. Balanced

5. Written Down and Shared

6. Visualize Nightly as if they are Already Achieved

7. Celebrate Victories and Failures

8. Replaced Each One as it is Achieved

The 7 Guidelines for Creating Desired Results

1. Important, Challenging, and Positive

Create important Desired Results. Otherwise, the smallest obstacle will prevent their achievement. If you do not "own" them, which is usually the case when they are chosen by someone else, your commitment will be lacking. You must have a PASSION for Creating Desired Results. Make them important and own them. As my father said, *"If you are not excited about a goal, forget about it."*

Create challenging Desired Results. Beating-the-odds creates huge levels of satisfaction, and makes further successes more likely. Desired Results which are unchallenging will not create a sense of victory when achieved. Beating someone at a game they have never played, for example, offers little satisfaction.

Create positive Desired Results. A 220-pound person should be striving to weigh 199 pounds, not to lose 21 pounds. Focus on what you do want, not on what you do not want.

2. Achievable

Create achievable Desired Results. If you set them too high, denial and avoidance will tend to follow. As you achieve them, set higher ones. Even if you only add slightly to your previous victories, you will continue to grow and win. It is important that you acknowledge all progress.

If you have not read a book in 10 years, starting with Tolstoy will ensure frustration. Start with something such as *"Jonathan Livingston Seagull"*. If you have not exercised in 20 years, a marathon may not be healthy. Start with a complete physical, then a light training regimen designed to get you to the point where you can complete a 5K run/walk. With consistency, you can easily build from there.

3. Specific, Measurable, Time Sensitive Events

Create specific Desired Results that are measurable, time-sensitive events. For example, replace "Making more money," with "Selling $1,000,000 worth of widgets by December 31st," so you have a specific target to celebrate.

Creating specific Desired Results requires you to focus on what you are going to achieve, and not on how you are going to achieve it. As such, your effectiveness will increase if you choose specific events such as completing a marathon or exceeding your quota. Activities such as running every day or phoning your existing clients weekly, are important and necessary, but are not the focus here.

4. Balanced

Always be in the process of Creating four (4) Desired Results ... one physical, one emotional, one mental, and one spiritual. Balance is essential for you to Create Desired Results that last.

PHYSICAL Desired Results:

Target something specific to do to improve your health, appearance, energy, diet, fitness, calmness, or simply to pamper yourself.

Examples: Achieving a specific weight, becoming smoke-free, completing a 5K walk/run, finishing a marathon, getting a physical or dental exam, treating yourself to a manicure or a massage, or getting a facial or pedicure.

EMOTIONAL Desired Results:

These are events that you are going to do "with" someone to improve the relationship (intimate, personal, social, family, or business), but not "for" them. They should be things the other person would enjoy or wants to accomplish; perhaps something that you have been avoiding.

Examples: Having a family outing, going on a date, phoning an old friend, having lunch with a parent, going to a ball-game with a buddy, taking a long walk with a child, or going on a get-away weekend or an intimate dinner with your spouse.

MENTAL Desired Results:

Here you choose things that will improve your self-esteem, knowledge, career, or prosperity; or just for fun (remember, *"All work and no play makes Jack a dull boy and Jane a dull girl."*).

Examples: Making a big sale, graduating from college, completing a continuing-education course, earning a specific sum of money, going on a vacation, exceeding your quota, reading a book, going hot-air ballooning, cleaning the garage, balancing your checkbook, going golfing, or finishing a project.

SPIRITUAL Desired Results:

Always strive to make a difference "with" your life, not just "in" your life. These are to be things you will do "for" someone else (unlike Emotional Desired Results, which are to be done "with" someone else), perhaps anonymously.

Examples: Donating money or volunteering time at a place of worship, giving away clothes or furniture to a women's shelter, reading to a shut-in, giving blood or platelets, picking up litter, or joining the church choir. The concept here is that pure "unconditional" giving always has a spiritual component.

5. Written Down and Shared

This is so simple, but most people avoid it. Create written Desired Results. Write them down, and keep them where you can see them on a daily basis.

As soon as you have chosen your Desired Results, show them to someone. If possible, make an agreement with that person to challenge you periodically on your progress. Pick someone who will support you, someone who has no stake in the outcome and who will not buy into any excuses. It is rarely a good idea for this person to be your spouse or business partner. They are too close.

6. Visualize Nightly as if they are Already Achieved

Perhaps the most important element of Creating Desired Results is to use your mind at night. Before getting ready for bed, find a comfortable place to sit. Do this sitting up because you may fall asleep if you lay down. Turn off the TV and, if possible, play symphonic music.

Close your eyes and visualize a structure ... a workshop. This is an imaginary place where you go to Create Desired Results. Inside this workshop is a wall-size TV or movie screen. This is the "Screen of Your Mind".

Every night, visualize each one of your Desired Results on the Screen of Your Mind. See them as if they had already been achieved earlier in the day. Then, imagine how that would have made you feel. Play a "Back-to-the-Future" mind-game with yourself. Make the feelings as real as possible.

When you are finished, prepare for bed. Before you fall asleep, let your mind dwell upon the images and the feelings you visualized earlier in your workshop on the Screen of Your Mind.

As you gain proficiency, your mind will provide you with insights and solutions as you need them. Keep a journal or tape-recorder beside your bed. This way you can make note of any insights or ideas you receive throughout the night, or the first thing in the morning when you wake up.

7. Celebrate Victories and Failures

Celebrate your victories, no matter how small. However, an important step in Creating Desired Results is to also celebrate your failures. By looking for something to learn from each failure, you increase your chances of future successes. That is worth celebrating. The bottom line is that if you do not celebrate your failures, you will be celebrating fewer successes ... guaranteed.

8. Replace Each One as it is Achieved

Whenever you achieve a Desired Result, immediately create a new one to take its place. Do not wait for all four to be completed. Long-term success depends on you keeping this as an active process.

The Fired Banker

"Ralph" was a banker in a major metropolis. He made a mistake and was fired. After several unsuccessful attempts to get a new job in banking, he came to me for coaching.

I told him, *"While banking is a large industry in this city, it is a small fraternity. Everyone knows what happened to you. Realistically, you either need to change careers, or move to a different city."* I thought this was a reasonable strategy.

Ralph disagreed, saying, *"My wife's family is here, and I don't want to leave banking."* He had drawn his line in the sand, so to speak. Now I had to help him come up with a solution.

First, I said, *"Let's start at the beginning. Clearly, by trying to say the right things to prospective employers, you are coming across as insecure and phony. You need to start using the power of your mind to overcome your insecurities. Tell me, how will it feel to finally get past all these problems and land a good job?"*

Ralph replied, *"It will be a relief. I will be excited. My wife will be ecstatic."*

"OK. Here's what I want you to do." I continued, *"Before going to bed at night, visualize yourself shaking the hand of someone who has just offered you the job you want ... and create those feelings of relief and excitement."*

"Nope," he responded. *"I have a better picture. Your father has always said that the mental picture must be exciting. Sure it will make me feel good to get back in banking, but what really excites me is the thought of finally getting a Porsche."*

I thought he was kidding. He was not. Nothing I could say would dissuade him. Finally, Ralph said, *"Look, for me to get a Porsche, I will have to have a hell of a job."* With this, I relented and helped him create his mental picture.

138

First I said, *"Close your eyes and imagine yourself sitting in your brand new Porsche."*

Ralph let out an audible sigh of pleasure. *"Now smell the interior. Sit on the leather seats. Adjust the mirror. Most importantly, I want you to notice how you are feeling."*

"Perfect," he responded with a grin.

"Turn on the engine and hear the sound. Feel the sensation as you begin to drive. Notice people turning to look." He was grinning ear to ear.

"That's it," I finally said. *"Do this every night until it is in your garage. I have never seen it fail. Remember, you have to create this mental picture and the resulting feeling of excitement ... as if it were real ... every night until it happens. No matter how long it takes."*

Ralph simply said, *"I'll do it."*

Less than three weeks later, he had his job. His employers agreed to finance his new car. It was a beauty. By using his mind before going to sleep, Ralph was able to change his attitude and thinking so he could interview from strength instead of desperation. This empowered him to land the job of his dreams.

The power of the human mind is beyond measure. By using your mind at night to visualize your desired results, you too can manifest your goals and dreams. It always works.

Ethics is about being accountable, honest,

and results oriented.

Creating Desired Results is a learned skill. Use the following exercise to get started. Long-term effectiveness will come with practice. Stick with it and you will find profound value in learning and using this tool.

EXERCISE #6 - Creating Desired Results

Create Four (4) Desired Results ... one physical, one emotional, one mental, one spiritual. Follow the preceding guidelines, and for the first few months, keep them short-term (to be achieved within 30 days or less). Once you have developed the discipline to Create "Short-Term" Desired Results, you will find it much easier to Create "Long-Term" Desired Results.

PHYSICAL – Create something for wellness or energy.
(i.e. Have my semi-annual dental exam)

_____

_____

_____ Date To Be Completed: _____

EMOTIONAL – Create something WITH someone.
(i.e. Taking my kids to the zoo)

_____

_____

_____ Date To Be Completed: _____

MENTAL – Create something for prosperity, knowledge or fun.
(i.e Exceeding my sales quota)

_____

_____

_____ Date To Be Completed: _____

SPIRITUAL – Create something FOR someone.
(i.e. Donating blood)

_____

_____

_____ Date To Be Completed: _____

ETHICS

**When what you THINK, what you SAY,
and what you DO are all the same.**

"Chance favors the prepared mind."
Louis Pasteur

"Live one day at a time, emphasizing ethics rather than rules."
Dr. Wayne W. Dyer

*"The first step in the evolution of ethics is
solidarity with other human beings."*
Dr. Albert Schweitzer

*"My life works in direct proportion to the
commitments I make and keep."*
James H. Quinn

BOTTOM LINE

When worried, risk failure, but speak your truth.

Focus on behaviors which calmly and kindly assure others that
you can be counted on to "Create Desired Results".

Somehow, some way – Get The Job Done.

ENTHUSIASM

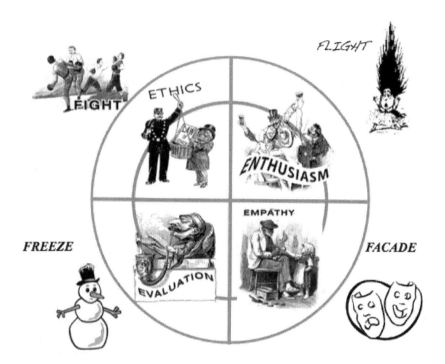

Seriousness is a Curable Disease

"The only thing more contagious than enthusiasm, is the lack of it."

James H. Quinn

CHAPTER 7

ENTHUSIASM
The Alternative to FREEZE

Whated by his initial... **W**hen stress triggers your FREEZE fear-based reaction, you bite your tongue, hide in your "cave," shut down, become unresponsive, and basically shut everyone out. You will become over-analytical and will not share your real thoughts or feelings ... until you have figured everything out, or are certain it is safe to do so. While the FREEZE fear-based reaction is often an attempt at self-protection, it is sometimes a conscious choice designed to protect others.

When you are shutting down, other people may or may not be your primary concern. While you may just be sorting out your own thoughts, you could also be trying to get back at someone by "freezing them out" and cutting off all communications. You might be trying to get the upper hand in negotiations by making the other party think you have lost interest in the deal, or you could be trying to protect someone else.

Regardless of your intent, the Freeze reaction can be threatening to others because they have no way of knowing what is really going on with you. They have to guess, and their assumptions can be much worse than the reality of whatever it is you are trying to hide.

> The FREEZE Fear-Based reaction often occurs with
> people who feel they are overwhelmed.
> Unfortunately, this can trigger impatience from others.

There seems to be no shortage of fear-based reactions in the world. A FREEZE fear-based reaction can often trigger a FIGHT, FLIGHT, FREEZE or FACADE from others. In fact, people may demonstrate their fear-based reactions even if they only perceive you to be isolating.

143

Perhaps you are not really shutting down or shutting them out, but are so focused on solving a problem that they feel ignored or taken for granted. If someone feels threatened they will react to you and the cycle begins. The problem you are hiding from will only grow larger as you hope, in vain, that it will just go away. Most of us take ourselves much too seriously when we are demonstrating the FREEZE fear-based reaction, and therefore procrastinate when faced with challenges. Spontaneity is missing.

The question becomes, *"How can I move into Enthusiasm, when I am in the middle of a FREEZE fear-based reaction?"* The answer: Tell people exactly how you are feeling and what you are thinking, before you figure out exactly what to say. In other words, learn to "think-out-loud".

Since the extreme FREEZE fear-based reaction is to become AVOIDANT, my recommendation for you to be enthusiastic may seem rash or even dangerous. This is difficult to argue with, because the FREEZE fear-based reaction has one purpose ... protection. Whether you are protecting your thoughts, feelings, family, business, or something else, it is all about protection.

The demonstration of the FREEZE fear-based reaction often has its roots in childhood or adolescence. Maybe you were told you were stupid when you blurted out an idea, or perhaps you were being spontaneous and were told to *"shut-up"*. You may have even heard the classic line, *"What will the neighbors think?"* Perhaps you were teased or bullied, and found safety by staying invisible. Regardless of the circumstance, you must have perceived at least some value in FREEZE fear-based reactions in order for this behavior to become a habit.

However secure it feels, the FREEZE reaction is still fear-based. Inappropriate people and challenging circumstances trigger your "head in the sand" or "nose to the grindstone" approaches to problems. You are only happy when circumstances are perfect, and they are never perfect. Bottom line, you give up control of your life when circumstances are in charge of your behavior.

**When tempted to Freeze,
take your power back with Enthusiasm.**

**Realize you are probably avoiding when you get
"Paralysis by Analysis".**

Just as a deer freezes in the headlights of an oncoming car, you are in danger when you analyze yourself into immobility. To place yourself in this kind of "voluntary" solitary confinement is to treat yourself in much the same way as society would treat the worst of criminals. There is an element of self-punishment involved when you isolate with the FREEZE fear-based reaction.

You do not have to be alone to isolate ... most of us have done so in a crowded room. In personal relationships, one person may interpret a lack of enthusiasm from their partner as a lack of affection. When someone feels rejected, unloved, or taken for granted, they may feel they have no choice but to look for another partner for warmth, attention, and affection. Destructive affairs and divorces can result from an unmet need for excitement.

Likewise, successful business relationships require enthusiastic interactions between management, employees, vendors, clients, and prospects. Timely responsiveness is often a signal to others of their value, whether there has been a problem or not. When there is a problem, people seem to have an inherent fear of the unknown, so even bad news is often better than no news at all.

An "Autistic" Adult

Some people are clear about their strengths and weaknesses, yet may still benefit from looking deeper to find gifts yet to be discovered and developed. Those with low self-esteem need to realize that they actually have value. Often, their gifts are found amongst the ruins of challenging life-circumstances.

"There is not anyone who cannot in some way add to Universe and contribute to humanity."

R. Buckminster Fuller

NOTE: Buckminster Fuller never put the word "the" in front of the word "universe". He said it would indicate that there are other universes.

When I first met Jane, she could not look anyone in the eye. She was in her own world, and nothing I could do could get her out of it. I began to wonder if she was an autistic adult.

It took two days of hard work before she was finally able to converse AND maintain eye-contact when conversing. Jane even began to sport a lovely smile. It was like watching a rose begin to blossom.

Then I told the group we were going to examine our childhoods to discover a few of our gifts. I said, *"Some of your higher qualities have been squashed, and you have longed for their return. Others, you may have never known."* At this point, Jane crossed her arms and legs, and again stared at the floor.

"What's up Jane?" I asked. Then I asked it twice more before I got a response.

"Nothing," She said without lifting her eyes.

"Come on Jane, please look at me and tell us what is going on," I asked.

Reluctantly, she looked at me and said, *"I cannot do what you are asking. I*

145

had an awful childhood, and I can't bear to think about it."

"*Okay, so what was it like?*" I seldom leave well enough alone. She looked away and did not answer.

"*Tell me why you are so shut down. What was it like?*" I repeated. Jane just stared at the floor.

"*If you will not even talk about it, then there is nothing to be accomplished here. I have to ask you to leave the class.*" While I did not want Jane to leave, I felt if she did not take a leap of faith now, it would matter little if she stayed.

Jane glared at me and said, "*You don't understand. I'm dying inside. I can't leave.*"

"*Fine. Then tell me why you are so shut down?*" I responded.

Jane said, "*Because I can't, and I won't.*"

"*Then you have to leave the class.*" I replied.

"*I can't leave. I need this class. I am dying.*" Jane was pleading now.

"*Then tell me why you are so shut down.*" I repeated.

"*You don't understand what you're asking. I have been in therapy for 10 years. My therapist has never gotten me to talk about my childhood, and you expect me to talk about it? Just like that?*" She was shouting.

"*Yes,*" was my reply.

Just like that, Jane opened up and told us of a childhood of isolation and sexual abuse. I will not go into the details, but it was the worst story of childhood abuse and neglect that I had ever heard. Basically, she was either ignored or molested. Jane remembered little else.

She was never praised, hugged, nurtured, or given a present of any sort. Jane was even ignored on her birthdays. In fact, she told us, "*The only thing I had to play with was a doll I made out of a few sticks and some rags. That doll was the only one I could talk to. That's how sick my childhood was. I finally left home at 15. No one even cared about that.*"

"*How wonderful,*" I responded. My tone was not sarcastic, but gentle. I was filled with admiration.

Jane did not understand, however, and asked, "*What's wonderful about that?*"

I said, "*You were treated as nothing. You were used, hurt, and isolated. Given the same circumstances, I doubt if I would have been as strong. I would have probably just wallowed in self-pity or jumped off of a building. But you chose to do something about it. You made a doll so you could have a friend. That is powerful. Tell me, what did you name her?*"

She was shocked, "*How did you know I named her?*"

"*Simple,*" I replied. "*Nobody with your courage and determination would not name the doll. How wonderful that you didn't kill yourself to escape your life of pain. Not only that, you left home and educated yourself. You have a good job, a nice home, and have spent 10 years in therapy trying to find yourself. Jane, you have greatness in you.*"

At first, Jane looked confused, but then she smiled. Had I asked her to define her best qualities, courage, determination, and greatness would not have been among her responses. Nevertheless, these qualities were obvious to me. I reached

146

her by simply sharing the truth about what I saw in her, and by giving her time to let it soak in.

After the two hours it had taken to get through this sharing, Jane was ready for anything. Talking about the rest of her life was easy. She had always dreamed of having a husband, but feared abandonment. She desperately longed for children, but feared her own childhood would become their destiny.

Jane also had ideas for her own business. Unfortunately, her feelings of unworthiness and fear of rejection had prevented her from making it a reality.

Talking about her childhood did not eliminate its pain, or her fears of being hurt again. While still terrified of the other people in the seminar, Jane suddenly became one of the leaders of the class. Living her life under a bushel basket had kept her safe, but it had suffocated her. Jane simply made a decision not to live that way anymore. From that time onward, she was the first to share, quickest to question, and was always willing to challenge others. It was a remarkable transformation.

I do not always see the end results of my seminars, but it is particularly gratifying to hear from people who have completely turned their lives around. Five years later, Jane wrote to me.

The letter spoke of my challenge for her to quit wallowing in self-pity and to do something with her life. Jane said that after class she entered and graduated from a business college, and then met and married a wonderful man. Not only that, her life-long dream of having a child had been fulfilled.

I went on to read that this terrified and unworthy woman had also created her own successful business. I will never forget her closing words …

Ross,

I promised myself I would write you when I felt

successful. Yesterday I hired my 100th employee

and I want you to know how successful I feel.

Thank you for believing in me.

Love, Jane

ENTHUSIASM

If you do not have enthusiasm, not much else matters. To live with enthusiasm is to have the energy to enjoy life. The personal rewards of living enthusiastically can be great. Problems become opportunities to create joy. Even daily exercise can become fun.

The Great Masters have never said,
"Seriousness To The World."

They have only and always said,
"Joy To The World."

The effect of enthusiasm on others is, perhaps, more significant. An unenthusiastic speech or sales-presentation is boring, regardless of the importance of its content. Conversely, even a poor speech has some impact when delivered with enthusiasm.

One of my favorite moments from a leadership seminar occurred when a dyslexic student took up a challenge to deliver a speech. No amount of practicing was helping. In fact, the more he worked on it, the worse his condition became.

I watched him fumble with sections of the speech he had already learned. I tried to help, but he became so frustrated he literally had trouble remembering his name. Finally, I told him as long as he was certain he was going to screw it up, he might as well do so with enthusiasm. Have some fun with it. *"After all,"* I told him, *"They pay Jim Carrey about $20,000,000 a movie to act dumb. Perhaps being perfect is not all it is cracked up to be."*

He thanked me and said he would make it fun. I was not certain if he was going to pull this off. Nonetheless, he was determined to give it his best shot.

However, from the moment he began, I knew it was going to be a wonderful speech. He had decided to change the beginning so the audience would understand what he was going through. He started with a joke. *"Have you heard of the new organization called DAM,"* he began. *"It stands for Mother's Against Dyslexia."* I could not believe it. This serious, self-conscious man was making fun of his disorder.

His speech was titled *"Courage"*, and was written by William Penn Patrick after he failed to become the Republican candidate in the 1966 race for the Governor of California (he lost to Ronald Reagan). Honestly, of the dozens of times I have heard it delivered, I have never seen it messed up so badly. Nonetheless, his speech was one of the best I have ever heard.

We were not laughing at him, we were laughing with him. He also made us cry. People hung on his every word, even when he had to try the same sentence several times. The courage he showed to us easily exceeded the courage he spoke of. His points got made, people understood his message, and we even had some fun.

In this story, it is important to note that even though this serious man did not eliminate his dyslexia or his terror, he was able to create enthusiasm and deliver his message in spite of that fact. He was entertaining and informative, and as motivational as you can get.

Certainly, enthusiasm alone is not enough. However, when those in leadership positions try to "motivate the troops", they had better do so enthusiastically.

> **Not only does leadership without enthusiasm usually fail,**
> **the lack of enthusiasm can create even bigger problems**
> **with an unmotivated staff or team.**

In a business world that moves at "Internet" speed, delays can be fatal. It is rare to find only one correct solution to a problem or challenge. Success in business often requires assumptions, risk, and enthusiasm.

Leaders, by definition, have followers. People are your barometer. Excellence is evident when you attract people who support, befriend, love, or endorse you.

The Problem: The FREEZE Fear-Based Reaction

When demonstrating the FREEZE fear-based reaction you become analyzing, isolated, and generally avoid others. Whether you are trying to get something right, figure something out, or avoid a relationship … you do not even speak until you have had the time to collect your thoughts. You are, or can appear to be, disconnected from others.

You will hear yourself internally asking "How" types of questions:
"How can you say that to me?"
"How can I do all of this?"

When Negatively Consumed With TASKS,
Your Primary Characteristic Tends to Be OVERWHELMED.

FREEZE

"I don't want to talk about it."
"In the time it takes to explain, I can do it myself."
"If you can't say something nice, don't say anything at all."

Other FREEZE Characteristics:

Anxious	Inward	Picky	Withdrawn	Apprehensive
Serious	Shameful	Tense	Isolated	Shut-Down

The Extreme FREEZE Fear-Based Reaction: AVOIDANT

Ask yourself,
"Do I generally avoid confrontation?"

150

The Solution: Add ENTHUSIASM

Make something happen. Focus on WHO to spend time with and WHEN you need to do so. You probably need to play, give others your full attention, and let people "IN" to your world. Quit worrying about HOW everything will work out. Planning your spontaneity can help remove some of the unknowns.

There are no problems that you can't make worse -- alone.

Balance yourself with ENTHUSIASM ...

Choose to Become:

Spontaneous   Energetic   Promoting   Open   Expressive
Positive   Exciting   Creative   Stimulating   Persuasive

Make TIME for RELATIONSHIPS

151

The Tool: Planned Spontaneity

Adherence to the old adage, *"Look before you leap"* has saved many people from making terrible decisions. The problem with the FREEZE fear-based reaction is the tendency to become too analyzing.

Yes, action without thinking can be dangerous, but thinking without action is nearly pointless. Sometimes, it is okay if everything is not perfect.

> **Occasionally, spontaneity is necessary.**
>
> **Every now and then you need to get a little crazy,**
>
> **or you will go nuts.**

One of my more analytical students came up with a solution, which worked well for him. Everything in this man's life was planned. His wife was originally attracted to him because of his stability.

Now however, she was beginning to see him as boring. He, on the other hand, was resenting her for trying to have fun with him when he was busy. He knew this was not smart, but could not bring himself to change.

He was in danger of losing the only woman he had ever loved. Try as he might, his projects always had to be finished before he could relax and enjoy himself. Since completing projects was not his strong suit, and starting new projects was never a problem, there was never any point of completion.

Then a solution occurred to him. He decided to treat his wife with the same energy as a project. He knew what she needed was some occasional fun, so he began to plan spontaneous fun things to do with her.

That's right, "Planned Spontaneity." He actually scheduled time to be spontaneous. It sounded ridiculous, but it worked.

Since he was impeccable with his appointments, once he booked some play time with his wife, it became a priority. He stopped resisting her.

Here is how it worked. At the beginning of the week, he would find a couple of hours of open time and book it as if it were a business appointment. Then, he would think about what kind of event he would create. He might plan to take his wife to a movie at a nearby theatre, go for a walk, or visit some friends. Once it was entered in his weekly planner, he could let it go.

When the scheduled time arrived, he would find his wife and tell her he wanted to take her to a movie. Whatever was showing was what they saw. Sure they saw some movies they hated, but sometimes they discovered a film they really loved, that would otherwise never have been seen.

This began to work so well, he decided to start creating fun in another way. This stiff, serious man began to teach himself how to juggle.

After a while he became pretty good at it. Now, when he finds himself in a long line at the supermarket, instead of reading the tabloids he starts to juggle something. He usually makes new friends in the process. Eventually, he even began to teach others to juggle.

Their marriage has healed. He is still a workaholic, but he is a lot more fun.

His wife never knows what to expect. Sometimes, he surprises her with a flower, dinner at a new restaurant, or even an unplanned trip. There is no longer any danger of her thinking of him as boring.

"Seriousness is a disease. Fortunately, it's curable."

James H. Quinn

EXERCISE #7 - Plan Something Spontaneous

1) Plan an hour of spontaneity, and book it into your schedule. This must be something fun, and you must do this WITH someone you care about (Journal the experience).

_____

_____

_____

_____

_____

_____

_____

_____

2) Identify something you are procrastinating or avoiding, and then DO IT RIGHT NOW ... with the energy and enthusiasm you would have for something you love to do. (Journal the experience).

_____

_____

_____

_____

_____

_____

_____

_____

_____

ENTHUSIASM

Always remember, without movement you stagnate.
So don't just sit there analyzing.

Do something!

"You can do anything if you have enthusiasm."
Henry Ford

"Nothing great was ever achieved without enthusiasm."
Ralph Waldo Emerson

"Enthusiasm is a vital element toward the individual success
of every man or woman."
Conrad Hilton

"Even if you're on the right track,
you'll get run over if you just sit there."
Will Rogers

BOTTOM LINE

When overwhelmed, instead of shutting down,

do something spontaneous ...

even if you have to plan it in advance.

EVALUATION

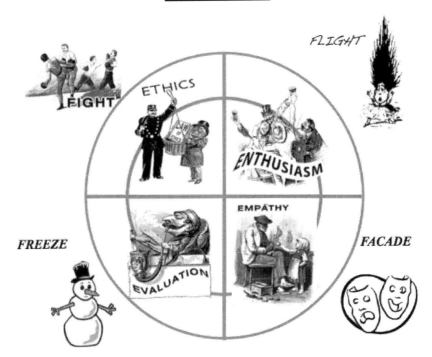

Misstakes r Larning Exspeariences

"Learning isn't a means to an end; it is an end in itself."

Robert A. Heinlein

CHAPTER 8

EVALUATION
The Alternative to FLIGHT

Whaen we find it impossible to face challenging situations, sometimes we have FLIGHT fear-based reactions. Examples would include running away from a relationship or abruptly quitting a job without a clear plan for a new one. Sometimes it manifests in the form of "running off at the mouth".

When you have a FLIGHT fear-based reaction, you may make comments as: *"I can't talk now"*; *"I'll take care of it later"*; *"It's not my fault I'm late"*; or *"Forget the plan, I have an idea"*. When you get frantic, other people's plans, goals, or needs are not your primary concern. You feel as though you are painted into a corner and are only interested in getting out. Unfortunately, your FLIGHT fear-based reaction often provides the justification for others to react to you.

If you are chronically late, then you already know that ignoring or avoiding problems does not make them go away, and procrastination invariably makes them worse. Problems cannot improve if they are not addressed. The FLIGHT fear-based reaction practically guarantees eventual disruption and chaos in the lives of others, who will then point to your behavior as their justification for attacking, shutting down, running away, or lying to you (Fight, Flight, Freeze or Facade).

The faster I go, the "be-hinder" I get.

People may react to you even if you just appear to be frantic. Perhaps you are firmly dug into your "Enthusiasm" mode. Not frazzled, but so intent on your problems that others feel unappreciated, used, or walked-on. If this threatens someone, it will begin the Reactive Cycle. They will react to you and then you react to them, and so on.

157

The human mind is quite possibly the most incredible creation in the universe. It allows us to evaluate our actions and make changes to our behaviors, in order to create beneficial results. Unfortunately, people will never find personal or business success as long as their mind-set is on scarcity, insecurity, unworthiness, lack, status quo, or any number of other issues.

We have all been taught to learn from our mistakes. Self-evaluation and the willingness to change are vital for personal and professional development. Unfortunately, for most people mistakes are not learning experiences, because they repeat non-productive, negative, and even destructive behaviors.

Evaluation begins with determination. You have to know that somehow you will become a successful salesperson, a good parent, a great manager, or a happy spouse. Failure and mistakes are not the problem. The problem is repeating them. The solution is learning from your mistakes, and doing something different the next time.

The best salespeople have one thing in common: after each sales call, whether successful or unsuccessful, they review their performance. These people evaluate the good and the bad to find things deserving acknowledgement, as well as to find things to improve.

If you want to get something different, you must do something different. Overcoming issues and learning from mistakes requires a mind-set for self-improvement. Without honest self-evaluation, the power of your mind will be reduced to rationalizing your own behaviors. Nothing will change. Your answers require a determination to grow.

"People are a lot like fruit.
When they're green, they grow. When they're ripe, they rot."

Bernard Beruce (Also the motto of Ray Kroc)

It has been observed that placing a piece of fruit in a jar that is tied down can capture monkeys. When a monkey reaches his hand into the jar, he discovers he cannot get his hand back out without dropping his prize. Instead of letting go of the fruit and running away as humans approach, he clings to it until he loses his freedom.

Most people are willing to try to make a job or marriage work, but really do not change what they are doing. They cling to behaviors that have already proven to be ineffective.

Reportedly, Thomas Edison tried thousands of experiments before his incandescent bulb actually worked. Notice, he tried thousands of different experiments. If Edison had repeated only the same experiment he would have been passed over by history. We all need to evaluate and learn from our failures in order to grow.

Ideas for evaluation typically come from taking an objective look at yourself, considering both the positive and negative feedback from others. One very effective way to do this is to take the time to journal a couple of paragraphs of observations, feelings, and insights at the end of each day. Afterwards, meditate on what you have written.

Without taking the time to reflect on potential solutions and keeping your priorities straight, you may hurry to an appointment, quit a job, or divorce a spouse in an attempt to avoid stress. Unfortunately, if your peace of mind is controlled by a circumstance, changing or controlling your circumstance only provides a temporary solution.

The Real Estate Salesman

Jim was usually the first person to arrive in his real estate office. This was a good thing since he always seemed to be behind in his paperwork. This morning he was meeting with a new client.

Bob spoke slowly and had difficulty describing the property he wished to purchase. Jim kept probing and questioning in an attempt to find out what this guy wanted, hardly waiting for Bob to finish his sentences. When the meeting was over, they made an appointment to go look at properties the next day after lunch.

That night, Jim poured over his Multiple-Listings book (this story takes place in the pre-computer era). He identified six different properties he felt would please his client.

The next day Jim had a long lunch with the local merchant's association. He did the best he could, but got to his office 20 minutes late for his appointment. Bob was not disturbed by his lateness, but seemed eager to get started. Jim, on the other hand, was already thinking ahead to his next commitment to meet with another client in two hours. They had to hurry if Bob wished to see all the properties.

At the first stop, Jim knew he was in trouble. Bob slowly wandered through the house examining everything in minute detail. His slow drawl was beginning to frustrate Jim. Finally, after unsuccessfully showing all six houses, they got back to the office. Jim found his next appointment waiting impatiently for him.

He made another appointment with Bob. This time Jim made the appointment his last of the day, so it would not get in the way of other clients. Jim stayed up later than usual, selecting eight more properties from his Multiple-Listing book.

True to form, and after an exhausting morning, Bob still had not found the home he was looking for. After five meetings, and four days of looking at homes, was about to cut his losses and tell Bob to work with another realtor. That is when he called me.

As I listened to Jim share his frustrations, an idea struck me. I suggested Jim give Bob his Multiple-Listing book, and let him take it home to study overnight.

Back then, in the era before the Internet, you never let the client look through the Multiple-Listing book as they would become overwhelmed with options. More importantly, it was not supposed to leave the realtor's office. Jim resisted my idea until he realized he had nothing to lose by giving it a try.

The next day Jim said, *"Bob, instead of running all over town again today, I'd like you to take my Multiple-Listing book home. I want you to look through it and see if you can find something I've been missing."* Bob's eyes lit up like a Christmas tree.

The following morning, Jim came into the office to find Bob waiting. He had found the perfect home and did not want to wait for someone else to get it first. Jim was a little perplexed. The home Bob had chosen was quite a bit more expensive than the upper limit he had been given. Jim would have already shown this home if he had known.

As they visited the property, Bob was as excited as a child opening presents. Everything was perfect and the sale closed quickly. It was one of Jim's largest sales of the year.

By taking the time to let Bob evaluate his own needs and desires, Jim allowed Bob to answer all of his own questions and objections in his own time. As a result, Jim never quite got around to the Flight reaction (dumping one prospect in favor of a better one).

Remember, when you are about to employ the Flight reaction, come from Evaluation instead. The answer, when frantic, is to stop and clear your mind. Your priorities will become clear and you will generally save more time than you had feared you might lose.

Lasting answers are to be found by changing yourself.

When stressed, calm down and do things differently than normal.

EVALUATION

When you find yourself frantically trying to accomplish more than can possibly be done, you may actually be fleeing from your problems instead of facing them. Here is a simple way to change that pattern. The next time you find yourself in crisis mode, stop and reflect on the reason you made a commitment, started a job, agreed to a project, or entered a relationship. Those desires or needs are probably going to go unfulfilled if you break your integrity, and you will eventually find yourself in the same frantic position in the next circumstance or relationship.

"Every time I left a marriage,
everything I was running from got to the next relationship
before I did."

A former student after her 4th divorce.

Since the extreme Flight reaction is to become histrionic (hysterical, frantic, and out of control), the choice to come from Evaluation seems impossible, and is resisted because of the immediate time crunch. This is difficult to argue with, because the Flight reaction has one purpose ... self-protection.

When confronted with problems, you would naturally tend toward Evaluation unless you have found some value in the Flight reaction. Perhaps by being frantic, you became difficult to pin down and, therefore, difficult to call on the carpet for broken agreements. Perhaps you found it easier to walk away from challenges and problems rather than face them. Others may have started solving your problems when you went into panic mode.

Whatever the reason, the Flight reaction is a form of fear-based living. If you choose to cling to this reaction, you are allowing other people to determine your peace. Unless you find a way to change, you will continue to react frantically when stressed. Begin by examining how you can keep your word or how to create what you originally wanted. Take the time to make plans. Make major changes slowly and with great consideration. Stop and prioritize what is important, and then finish one thing at a time ... especially when it seems impossible to do so.

The Problem: The FLIGHT Fear-Based Reaction

When demonstrating a FLIGHT fear-based reaction you panic, make excuses, rush, motor-mouth, or interrupt others. Whether you are trying to find something for someone, make it to an appointment, or get away from someone ... you say the first thing that comes to your mind. You are, or can appear to be, not listening to anyone else.

You will hear yourself asking "Who?" or "When?" types of questions:
"Who do you think you are?"... "Who is going to be there?"
"When is the appointment?"... "When will you finally start listening to me?"

When Negatively Consumed With RELATIONSHIPS,
Your Primary Characteristic Tends to Be FRANTIC.

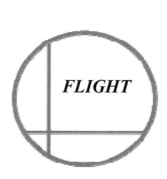 

FLIGHT

"I don't have to take this, I'm out of here."
"Don't worry about it. I'll take care of it later."
"I've got too much to do and not enough time to do it."

Other FLIGHT Characteristics:

Distracted   Overwhelming   Harried   Panicked   Hyperactive
Impulsive   Hurried   Excitable   Pushy   Scattered

The Extreme FLIGHT Fear-Based Reaction: HISTRIONIC (Frenzied)

Ask yourself,
"Do I easily become panicked?"

162

The Solution: Add EVALUATION

Solicit ideas and feedback, and actually consider what you hear. Take the time to figure out HOW you created this stress, and HOW to prevent it in the future. You need to slow down, give others information, and let others help you. Remember the moral from Aesop's Fable, The Tortoise and the Hare ... *"Slow and steady wins the race."*

> *"When your stomach disputes you,*
> *lie down and pacify it with cool thoughts."*
>
> Satchel Paige

Balance yourself with EVALUATION ...

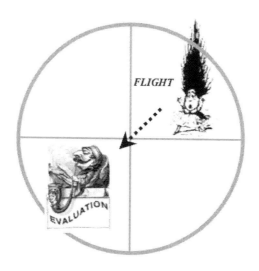

Choose to Become:

Patient   Diligent   Reliable   Industrious   Methodical

Detailed   Persistent   Integral   Precise   Deliberate

Focus on TASKS and COMMITMENTS

163

The Tool: Centering

The reduction, "re-direction," or elimination of stress is essential in the modern world. There are many ways to accomplish this objective. Examples include prayer, exercise, sports, gardening, and hobbies; as well as meditations such as Centering, Christian Contemplation, and Transcendental Meditation.

Almost any discipline is effective, as long as it gets your mind off your troubles. Two things which do NOT work are 1) becoming consumed with your problems, or 2) avoiding them with drugs, alcohol, shopping, food, work-a-holism, or any escapist/avoid-ant activities.

I practice and teach a safe, simple, and effective "Rainbow Centering" technique. This powerful tool aids people in Stress Reduction when used for SELF-DISCOVERY in the morning; and for CREATING DESIRED RESULTS (Chapter 6, page 134), when used in the evening.

During the day, in periods of high stress, even one or two minutes of centering can be highly beneficial. Quiet spots may be hard to come by, but there are private restrooms almost everywhere (and they are quiet too).

If you practice the Rainbow Centering technique twice a day for 21 days, it will begin to feel as natural as brushing your teeth, putting on make-up, or shaving. You will find that by centering in this manner for about 15 minutes in the morning and 15 minutes in the evening (but even 5 minutes has great value), that you will increase your personal and professional effectiveness dramatically.

EXERCISE #8 - CENTERING

Sit with your feet flat on the floor. Move your feet slightly forward so your ankles are directly beneath your knees. Open your palms, as if you are holding a huge beach ball on your lap. Lift your chin so that your eyes are elevated slightly above the horizon. Push your shoulders back and straighten your spine.

If you prefer to lie down, position yourself as follows to maximize your results and prevent yourself from falling asleep. Lay on the floor, not on your bed (old sleep patterns are difficult to overcome). Lift your knees, keeping your feet flat on the floor. Arch your neck slightly, as if to look at the top of the wall behind you. Spread your arms out from your sides, just slightly apart from your torso. Lift one hand, with your elbow remaining on the ground. If your hand starts getting heavy, simply change hands.

You may find it beneficial to make a recording of the following procedure. I also recommend that you play soft, symphonic music, or sounds from nature to help create a supportive environment. Several different Centering CDs are available on my website: www.LoveBasedLeader.com.

Step One -- Relax Your Physical Body:

Close your eyes and visualize something RED from nature, perhaps, an apple or a rose. Use this color as a mental trigger device to relax your physical body. While keeping the color red in your mind's eye, relax every muscle in your body. Start from the top of your head and finish with your feet. Imagine yourself with no muscles or joints.

Step Two -- Release Your Emotions:

Visualize something ORANGE from nature, such as an orange or a flower. This color is the mental trigger device to release and let go of negativity. While keeping the color orange in your mind's eye, feel yourself getting lighter as you "watch" negative emotions such as resentment flow away.

Step Three -- Calm Your Mind:

Visualize something YELLOW from nature, perhaps a banana or a flower. Use this color as a mental trigger device to calm and still your mind. While visualizing the color yellow, slow your mind down. Clear your mind of all negative thoughts, and watch them float away like yellow clouds.

Step Four -- Sense Inner Peace:

Visualize something GREEN from nature, such as a lawn or a tree. Use this color as a mental trigger device to sense inner peace. Allow yourself to experience an indwelling presence of peace and serenity.

Step Five -- Feel Love:

Then visualize something BLUE from nature, perhaps the sky or a sapphire. This color is the mental trigger device for feeling the emotion of love. As you visualize the color blue in your mind's eye, feel love radiating to you and through you to others, as if you are a living conduit of love.

Step Six -- Seek Wisdom:

Visualize something PURPLE from nature, such as the deep indigo color of eggplants or grapes. This color is the mental trigger device for aspiration. While keeping the color purple in your mind's eye, seek out the unique genius within yourself and listen for insights regarding your gifts and true purpose.

Step Seven -- Be Centered:

Visualize something VIOLET from nature, perhaps orchids or tiny violets. Use this color as the mental trigger device for being centered. Accept that all people have gifts, value, and purpose ... regardless of whether they realize it or not.

165

Step Eight (Mornings) -- Listen to Your Inner Voice:

Experience whatever you are led to experience. Allow yourself to be still and quiet for several minutes. Answers and ideas may come to mind, but if not, just use the time to relax. If you find it difficult to do nothing with your mind, then visualize yourself as a child freely demonstrating your gifts (such as Boldness, Enthusiasm, Determination, or Caring) to others. Either way, just let go.

Step Eight (Evenings) -- Creating Desired Results:

Imagine you are entering your Workshop and then visualize each of your Desired Results on the Screen of Your Mind. Remember to see each result as if it is already achieved, and to create the feelings you would have had ... if it actually had been achieved (see Chapter 6, Page 137 – **Visualize Nightly as if they are Already Achieved**).

Step Nine -- Ending:

State the following affirmation:

Each day, in every way, I am getting better and better and better.

Then, slowly visualize the seven colors of the rainbow
in reverse sequence:

Starting with the inner most color Violet,
moving upwards and out to Purple,
next to Blue, then Green,
next Yellow, Orange, and Red.

As you open your eyes, repeat the following:

I open my eyes and I am wide awake.
I am revitalized, refreshed, and in tune with life.
I am enlightened. I am enriched. I am enthused. I am energized.

I am. I just am.

EVALUATION

Listen to your unique "Genius" within.

"The intuitive mind is a sacred gift,
and the rational mind is a faithful servant."
Albert Einstein

"Look before you leap."
Samuel Butler

"Balance lives in the present. Bring yourself back to the now."
Oprah Winfrey

"And he awoke and rebuked the wind and said to the sea,
"Peace! Be still!'."
Jesus, Mark 4:39 English Standard Version of The Holy Bible

BOTTOM LINE

When overwhelmed, instead of getting hyper,

take the time to "Center" and get clear on your priorities.

EMPATHY

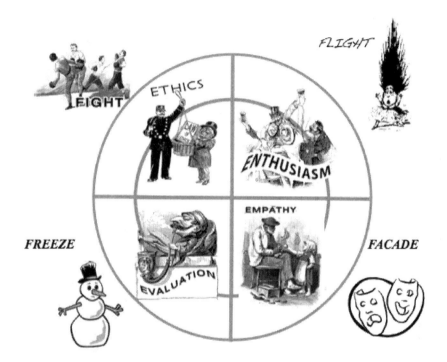

Acceptance Not Judgment

*"People don't care how much you know,
until they know how much you care."*

Unknown

CHAPTER 9

EMPATHY
The Alternative to FIGHT

W hen you have a FIGHT fear-based reaction, you tend to be brutally honest, critical, or sarcastic. It is generally triggered by judgmental or self-righteous thoughts and feelings, and can take the form of sarcasm, criticism, verbal abuse, and worse. *"I don't get mad, I get even,"* could be your motto.

While a FIGHT fear-based reaction is usually either an attempt at self-protection, or a punishment dealt out to others, it is often motivated by the desire to protect others from themselves. You can justify attacking the very people you care about, and blame them for it. *"This is for your own good"; "This is going to hurt me more than it's going to hurt you,"; "I'm only yelling at you because you were yelling at me!"* are phrases you may have used to justify yourself.

Your FIGHT fear-based reactions often are triggered by anger, which can lead you to make truthful but negative comments such as, *"You are a liar"; "Do it this way, or you're fired"; "Your problem is you only think of yourself"; "I can't trust you"* or *"I'm tired of your excuses."*

When you are angry and demonstrating the FIGHT fear-based reaction by telling someone off or putting them down, the feelings and needs of your target are not your primary concern ... you just want to tell the truth. Unfortunately, your FIGHT fear-based reaction provides justification for the fear-based reactions of others, which will begin or escalate the Reactive Cycle (page 63).

> *"Never get angry. Never make a threat. Reason with people."*
>
> Don Corleone, The Godfather

It is easy to see how resistance and resentment are typical reactions to the FIGHT fear-based reaction. Nobody likes to be yelled at, bullied, or pushed around, even when his or her own reactive behavior may have triggered an angry reaction in turn. No matter how justified your outrage, people will tend to react badly to you when they see you as angry or judgmental. The Fight reaction practically guarantees you will be attacked, ignored, lied to, or abandoned.

Using Empathy to overcome this reaction can be difficult, as you must have perceived your FIGHT Reactions as valuable in order to have developed them in the first place. Nevertheless, Empathy is the solution for overcoming FIGHT fear-based reactions.

However strong it appears now, the FIGHT reaction is still fear-based. Other people trigger your negative behaviors. If they treat you right, you do not attack. If they do not treat you right, you attack. The bottom line is you are at the mercy of how other people treat you. You are not in charge of yourself when you demonstrate the Fight Reaction.

The irony is that you could not have developed FIGHT fear-based reactions unless you were very sensitive. Whether you remember it or not, you would not be reacting in such a manner unless you were hurt in the past. When you showed kindness, you might have been laughed at. There may have been a time you tried to give love, but were rejected. Perhaps you were creative, but were criticized. Maybe you needed someone who abandoned you. Regardless, you eventually felt a need to protect yourself. This is where the FIGHT fear-based reaction started.

Then it got stronger with success. Perhaps getting mad stopped people from picking on you, or arrogance helped you to bury hurt from a relationship gone bad. Maybe you were even taught that *"nice guys finish last."*

The FIGHT fear-based reaction has one purpose … to protect you. But, if you have ever yelled in frustration, *"If I've told you once, I've told you a thousand times,"* then you know how ineffective the FIGHT fear-based reaction truly is. Otherwise, your point would have been made long before you shouted it 999 times.

If you don't change what you are doing,

you are going to end up where you are heading.

The extreme FIGHT fear-based reaction is to become paranoid. Is that where you really want to end up?

The answer, when you are engaged in the FIGHT fear-based reaction, is to say exactly what you were going to snarl or shout, but do so with kindness and respect. If what you are trying to communicate is important, say it in a way in which the intended receiver will hear it. Simply change HOW you say it, by adding Empathy.

EMPATHY

To lack empathy is to deny your own need for others. Abraham Maslow, in his famous "Hierarchy of Needs" defined one of the key motivators of human behavior as the "belonging need" or the need for people. Friendships, marriages, co-workers, religious acquaintances, comrades in arms, teammates, siblings, and anyone having similar interests can fill this need.

All relationships have problems. With empathy, you do not start with the premise that the other person is an idiot, incompetent, or evil, just because you do not understand them. To do that is to guarantee your attempts to reach them, much less help them, will fail. You will not lead, as your reactions will be counter-productive to your aims and desires.

> **Empathy is the ability to relate to the feelings, emotions, thoughts, actions, and circumstances of others.**

Even with empathy, you may not always comprehend why someone is behaving in a non-constructive or destructive manner. But you will understand that it somehow makes sense to them.

Many confuse empathy with sympathy, but they are very different. Just as with a sympathetic toothache, when the pain from one tooth feels like it is also coming from another tooth, a sympathetic person actually feels the pain of another. For example, a friend loses a job and is resenting his or her manager, so you resent the boss as well. If you feel bad, I feel bad. *"I can't understand why your boss fired you. He is such an idiot."*

With empathy, on the other hand, you understand how another feels, but it does not make you feel the same way. *"I understand your resentment for your boss, but resenting him is eating you up inside."*

Love-based leaders do not take advantage of, ignore, or attack other people. They realize there will be consequences to their fear-based reactions. Accordingly, love-based leaders know that their reactions could cause valuable people to leave the relationship, and that dangerous ones could mount a counter-attack. Either way, they realize that a price will be paid.

The Problem: The FIGHT Fear-Based Reaction

When demonstrating a FIGHT fear-based reaction you give ultimatums, get sarcastic, become vengeful, yell, or even attack someone physically. Whether you are actively seeking to fix something, finish something, or punish someone ... you say exactly what you mean. You are, or can appear to be, unconcerned about the needs and feelings of others.

You will hear yourself asking "What?" types of questions:
"What's your problem?" ... "What are you going to do about it?"

When Negatively Consumed With RESULTS,
Your Primary Characteristic Tends to Be JUDGMENTAL.

"I don't get mad, I get even."
"If you want something done right, you've got to do it yourself."
"The end justifies the means."

Other FIGHT Characteristics:

Aggressive   Manipulative   Arrogant   Sarcastic   Critical
Demanding   Intimidating   Insensitive   Offensive   Argumentative

The Extreme FIGHT Fear-Based Reaction: PARANOID

Ask yourself,
"Do I tend to be blunt with criticism and judgment?"

172

The Solution: Add EMPATHY

Avoid judgment and telling people WHAT to do. Look for something to acknowledge. Take the time to explain WHY to others, or to ask WHY type questions. You need to forgive, give others courtesy, and let people give to you. Remember, it isn't what you say; it's how you say it.

"Tenderness and kindness are not signs of weakness and despair, but manifestations of strength and resolutions."

Kahlil Gibran "The Prophet"

Balance yourself with EMPATHY ...

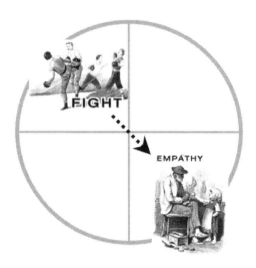

Choose to Become:

Courteous   Supportive   Cooperative   Responsive   Kind
Friendly   Accommodating   Nurturing   Compassionate   Accepting

---

Focus on EMOTIONS and FEELINGS

173

The New Car Dealer

Tom was the owner of the largest car dealership in the city, but he had a problem. Tom had a good location, superb mechanics, excellent sales-people, but an inconsistent body shop. He finally found a small operation nearby, with an owner-operator who did impeccable work. However, it was not under his direct control. As a hands-on manager, Tom wanted to have the body work done in-house.

After several years resisting Tom's offers to work for him, the body shop man relented, and agreed to work for the dealership. It was a classic win-win agreement: Tom got an employee he could be proud of; his new employee got a state-of-the-art facility, and was given a free hand to run it as he saw fit.

Shortly afterwards, Tom's best friend had an accident with his new car. He needed it repaired for his anniversary the following weekend. He assured his friend that not only would the car be ready, but also that his new employee would make it look like new.

Three days later, the repair work had not even been started. Apparently, his new employee had been too busy setting up his new shop. Tom was furious!

Tom's normal reaction would have been to turn tyrannical and perhaps even fire the man ... and all the effort he put in to hiring this worker would be lost. Tom knew that if he gave in to his Fight Reaction, his employee might simply quit and return to self-employment. Tom had to find another way to approach the problem.

Tom shifted to Empathy. He had already told his employee WHAT he needed; now he had to tell him WHY. Tom decided to take some time to sit down with his new employee and get to know him better.

At first, they spent time discussing the arrangements of their new "partnership." Tom asked his employee how he felt about his new workshop, taking the time to really listen to his excitement and concerns. Eventually Tom asked, *"If you were me, and had to go tell a friend that his car would not be ready for his anniversary, after you had promised him it would be ready, how would it make you feel?"*

Tom could see his new employee's eyes light up in understanding. He nodded, wished the man a pleasant afternoon, and then left him alone.

Without ultimatums or threats, the body shop man immediately got to work fixing the car. Not only that, he went above and beyond the call of duty by pulling several late-night shifts to make sure the work was done perfectly, and on time.

By painting an emotional picture that was easy to understand, Tom was able to relate his needs to his employee. The car was finished with time to spare, and the relationship, so close to a bad start, was firmly established with mutual respect.

The Tool: The Trust Formula

At the core of your creation or enhancement of your effectiveness as a love-based leader is the ability to inspire trust, and thus gain support from others. In relationships, people who trust you will listen to you, open up to you, date you, befriend you, endorse you, and will generally want to spend time with you. In business, they will buy from you, hire you, promote you, recommend you, work hard for you, and will want you on their team. In politics, people who trust you will volunteer time, give you their vote, spread your message, and make campaign contributions.

There is a formula that can make gaining trust much easier. Consistent use of this formula has enabled many of my students to reach previously unreachable people. Of course, nothing guarantees how others will respond, but the "Trust Formula" will definitely increase your odds of a positive response.

When you demonstrate a fear-based reaction to others, you actually give them an excuse to react to you. Eventually, they will grow to expect your negative behavior and pre-act to you. The love-based leader strives to remove these excuses by refusing to react in the first place.

There is an effective technique that empowers you to stay in control. I call this tool the "Trust Formula." When you are about to react or pre-act with any negative behavior, simply stop and think the following sentence:

The Trust Formula

"I love you and I accept you,
even though I don't understand you,
and I forgive you."

Here is how it works. When you are feeling angry and judgmental, and are about to attack someone, stop and just think the formula's exact words. This pause will give you a chance to re-establish self-control, and choose an Empathetic alternative to a fear-based reaction.

Unfortunately, the loss of self-control is all too common. If you are like me, you may have even reacted negatively when you first read this formula (see how easy it is to get you to react?). I actually laughed when I first heard it. I thought, *"If you do this formula when people are treating you wrong, they will eat you alive. You have opened the door to continued abuse."*

A typical reaction is to resist using the Trust Formula, even in a Level-1 Negative Circumstance (i.e. spilt milk). Acceptance and honor are even more difficult to express following a Level-2 Negative Circumstance such as a firing, a car accident, or a crime. However, forgiveness seems to be the rarest of commodities when there is a Level-3 Negative Circumstance ... a death caused by alcohol, drugs, physical abuse, medical malpractice, murder, war, or terrorism.

Nevertheless, this formula will help you to create trust … and give you a side benefit of reduced stress. You do not have to believe it. You do not have to like it. You do not even have to feel it. Just try it. What do you have to lose?

With the exception of love-based leaders such as Jesus Christ, Mahatma Gandhi, Mother Teresa, and Martin Luther King, Jr., very few people have ever lived their lives demonstrating something like the Trust Formula. When something goes wrong, most of us seem to employ the following "Distrust" Formula:

The "Distrust" Formula

I don't understand you.
Therefore, I don't accept you,
I don't love you, and I resist you.

How much of that kind of attitude do you see on a daily basis over "little" Level-1 Negative Circumstances at home, on the highway, at work, in restaurants, in stores, and even in places of worship? The question is not, *"Does the Trust Formula work?"* The question should be, *"What is the "Distrust" Formula doing to our children, our families, our business relationships, our communities, our country, and our world?"*

Fear-based reactors justify negative behaviors when they are afraid. Whether by Fight, Flight, Freeze, or Facade they strive to control others. Their attitude to others is, *"You are the problem. If you would just change what you are doing, then there would be no problem."* In essence, they seek to create peace by trying to make others responsible for solving problems.

Conversely, love-based leaders, by using the Trust Formula, choose to maintain self-control when afraid. Their attitude to others is, *"I don't understand you, but I do understand that if you were not threatened, you would not be reacting. It is in my own best interest to change whatever it is I am doing (or am perceived as doing), and thus remove the threat."* They seek to create peace by being responsible for solving problems themselves.

Notice that both groups are interested in the same result. However, by trying to control others, fear-based reactors are losing effectiveness.

The goal is to become so good at it that you can implement the Trust Formula the instant you sense that you are about to have a fear-based reaction. But, you will often see results when you suddenly realize that you are in the middle of a fear-based reaction, and shift to the Trust Formula instead of continuing to react. People seem to notice, and respond to, your change of attitude.

The Trust Formula is not just a philosophy. It works. But it will only work if you use it.

Using the Trust Formula

The Trust Formula is designed to help you to gain self-control, and definitely not as a tool to control other people. Self-control demonstrates to others that you can be trusted. Most people have to practice this many times before they see results. Nevertheless, they always see results, usually more quickly and profoundly than they expect ... whether they demonstrate the Trust Formula before, or during, a fear-based reaction.

So, when you have been taken advantage of in business, before you demonstrate a fear-based reaction, just stop and think, *"I love you and I accept you, even though I don't understand you, and I forgive you."*

If your spouse pushes your buttons, and you are about to attack, bite your lip and say to yourself, *"I love you and I accept you, even though I don't understand you, and I forgive you."*

When your son, daughter, or parents frustrate you with an obvious lie, before you explode just think, *"I love you and I accept you, even though I don't understand you, and I forgive you."*

When you encounter challenging or negative clients, co-workers, employees, or employers in the workplace, just say to them in your mind, *"I love you and I accept you, even though I don't understand you, and I forgive you."*

Whenever something especially negative occurs and you are strongly tempted to employ a FIGHT fear-based reaction, use the "Special" Trust Formula:

The Special Trust Formula

I love you and I accept you,
***ESPECIALLY** when I don't understand you,*
and I forgive you.

Whether you begin practicing The Trust Formula or The "Special" Trust Formula, if you want results then begin now, and stay with it. By practicing it on Level-1 Negative Circumstances, and by practicing it on Level-2 Negative Circumstances, you will develop the expertise to handle Level-3 Negative Circumstances. Sooner than you imagine, you will see results.

IMPORTANT: Do not speak The Trust Formula out loud. It can have strange effect on a spouse or a boss when, in the middle of an argument, you say to them, *"I love you and I accept you, even though I don't understand you, and I forgive you."* It can come across as self-righteous and patronizing, and can make things worse. Nevertheless, as you are about to read, there are exceptions to this rule.

177

The Crisis Negotiator

Dear Ross,

Last night at 9:15 pm, I was dispatched to the 911 Center. The Crisis Negotiation Team, of which I am a member and negotiator, had been paged out to deal with a man in the county who had shot at officers. He had barricaded himself in his house, and would not come out. He was, however, willing to speak on the phone.

At 9:45 pm, the primary negotiator began talking with the man in crisis, with me listening in on another headset. My assignment for the incident, as the second chair negotiator, was to listen to the dialog and feed ideas to the primary negotiator.

After letting him vent for several minutes, I recognized that the man in crisis was a sad 52 year-old man who was just tired of the world and who DID NOT like authority figures, especially police. He had a treatable medical condition, but insurance issues had prevented him from getting the medical attention he needed.

It turned out he did not like women because of how he had been treated by them in the past. The primary negotiator, a female, did an outstanding job at putting him at ease. We went back and forth for approximately one hour trying to build a rapport with him, to get him to come out of the house peacefully.

Then we hit a wall. He just wanted to be left alone, and was not going to be coming out. But, after shooting at police officers with a shotgun, we could not just leave. He was getting irritated that we would not just go away.

We could not leave until he came out. We knew that he had weapons in the house, and we did not want to risk sending SWAT in after him. If he were to have a shotgun trained on his front door, one of our friends could be shot in the process. Talking him out was our only option.

At that point, I had a WOW moment. I thought back to my BreakThrough class with you, and imagined him as if he were one of our classmates sharing about his life. I thought about some of the things you taught us, and how I could apply those things to create a win-win situation. At that moment, it hit me.

I wrote a quick variation of *"I love you and I accept you, even though I don't understand you,"* and handed it to the primary. The primary shrugged and read word for word: *"I appreciate the situation you are in. I accept you for who you are, even though I do not understand why you have taken these measures. Can you please help me to understand what it is in your past that is really preventing you from coming out of the house to talk to us in person?"*

The man said, *"OK, I'll tell you,"* and he did. He talked for about

10 minutes on how he had issues with police. He was afraid of coming out because he thought he would get beat up.

The next thing I wrote on the pad was, *"I appreciate you for sharing that with me. I promise you that if you come out and talk to us, you will not get hurt."* Again, she read it word for word. He went silent for several minutes, but we could tell that the line was still open.

Then, out of the blue, he talked about how he used to be a bull rider. The primary asked him if he was a good bull rider. He said he was pretty good, and had won a few competitions when he was younger.

I grabbed the pad and wrote, **WIN - WIN**. The primary looked at me and smiled. SHE GOT IT. Her next question was, *"So, how did it feel when you won?"* He replied positively and talked for another couple of minutes on how it felt.

I then smiled from ear-to-ear and whispered to the primary, *"Did you feel in control riding the bull when you won?"* When the primary asked him that question, he stated that he did.

Now it was like she was reading my mind. She smiled at me and told him that he seems like a man who wants to be in control. He agreed. She then told him that it appears that several things that have taken place in his life have caused him to feel like he is not in control. Again he agreed.

She continued, *"You can take control now by coming out and talking to us, or lose control if we have to come in after you. Why don't you be the winner you were as a bull rider. Apply those good times and feelings, and take control by coming out to talk to us. If you do that, we all win!"*

The phone went silent. The primary kept asking him if he was there, and if he was alright. About 5 minutes went by with no contact. We were getting worried.

Then we got a call from the Negotiations Commander at the scene that he had just walked out of the house and surrendered peacefully. I about passed out, laughed, smiled, jumped up and down and cried.

Yes, I went through every possible emotion in about 5 seconds. WOW. What you taught me worked in my professional life as well as it has worked in my personal life. What an incredible tool.

So, you can take pride that YOU had a part in saving a man's life last night. I truly feel that the turning point in the negotiation was when my thoughts turned to you for help in getting through this.

Had I not, the outcome could have been very different and possibly even fatal. You provided me with the tools to create the ultimate win-win situation ... the saving of a man's life.

Thank you.
Love, Mike
(Last name and city withheld by request)

Using the Trust Formula on Yourself

It is one thing to forgive others. It is another thing altogether to forgive yourself. Have you ever felt ashamed about something you did or did not do? The biggest damages we incur are often self-inflected, so learning to forgive yourself is critical if you want to be a love-based leader.

When you demonstrate a fear-based reaction and later feel badly, there is a strong likelihood of spiraling deeper into the Reactive Cycle (page 63). Beating on yourself is just as ineffective as beating on someone else.

The truth? Old habits die hard. Be aware of this fact, and be prepared to use the Trust Formula on yourself. Here is how it works.

Whenever you react to someone and then start to regret your actions, instead of thinking, *"I should have"*, or *"I shouldn't have"* simply say the Trust Formula to yourself.

I love myself and I accept myself,
even though I don't understand myself,
and I forgive myself.

Of all the things I teach, this one simple tool seems to create more positive results than you can imagine. We go through life trying to figure everyone else out. Yet how many of us truly understand ourselves?

Unfortunately, from time to time, all of us react in ways that we are ashamed of. When this occurs, the tendency is to "beat yourself up" or "put yourself down." The result of such actions is to damage your own self-worth.

Conversely, each time you turn the Trust Formula inward, you actually take a step towards a stronger self-worth. And if there is one thing you will need to create personal and professional results in your life, it is self-worth.

With a positive and healthy self-worth, you will become your own best friend, and will be able to bounce back from anything. Without a positive and healthy self-worth, you will become your own worst enemy, and just about anything will cause you to crush yourself.

Practice using the Trust Formula on yourself. Practice on little things. Practice on big things. You will not find a better tool to build your strength.

EXERCISE #9 - Creating Trust

In a normal day, you probably will not have any Level-3 or Level-2 Negative Circumstances (death or destruction). You will, however, have many Level-1 Negative Circumstances (inconveniences). Face it, if you cannot control yourself when something small goes wrong, it is unlikely you will spontaneously develop into a love-based leader when big things go wrong. Practice on small stuff.

1) Over the next 24 hours, every time something goes wrong and you are about to demonstrate a fear-based reaction, practice using the Trust Formula first, and see what happens. Keep track of each encounter. If someone cuts you off on the freeway, steals your briefcase, serves you the wrong food, spills milk, gossips, criticizes you, laughs at you, or is just plain mean, just pause and use the Trust Formula BEFORE you react. Afterward, go ahead and react if you are still so inclined. Just get used to pausing before you do so. Do this at least 5 times. **Journal your insights**:

_____

_____

_____

_____

_____

_____

2) Over the next 24 hours, every time something goes wrong, and you automatically demonstrate a fear-based reaction, practice using the Trust Formula on **yourself** afterwards and see what happens (whether you regret the reaction or not). Just as in the first exercise on this page, keep track of each encounter. Look for patterns. Do this at least 5 times. **Journal your insights**:

_____

_____

_____

_____

_____

181

"For to win one hundred victories in one hundred battles, is not the acme of skill.

To subdue the enemy without fighting is the acme of skill."

Sun Tzu (The Art of War)

EMPATHY

Compassion for others is a strength. Use it.

"We have been created to love and be loved."
Mother Teresa

"The greatest thing you'll ever learn is just to love and be loved in return."
Toulouse Lautrec (from the movie, Moulin Rouge)

"Non-violence leads to the highest ethics, which is the goal of all evolution."
Thomas Edison

"Father forgive them, for they know not what they do."
Jesus, Luke 23:24, The Holy Bible

BOTTOM LINE

Use the **Trust Formula** BEFORE or DURING
each of your Fear-Based Reactions.

*"I love you and I accept you,
even though I don't understand you,
and I forgive you."*

Use the **Trust Formula** on yourself AFTER
each of your Fear-Based Reactions.

*"I love myself and I accept myself,
even though I don't understand myself,
and I forgive myself."*

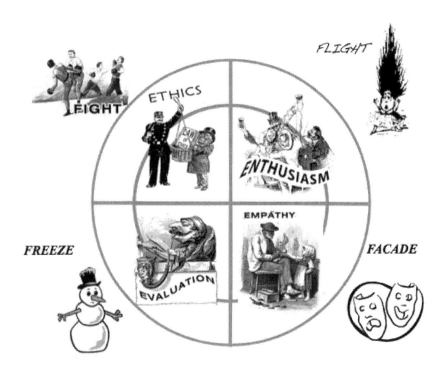

CHAPTER 10

The Four Personality Styles

Throughout history, there have been countless behavioral theories. They have come from religious, astrological, philosophical, psychological, psychiatric, and educational arenas. From Aristotle to Dr. Phil McGraw, there have been many who have spent their lifetimes on quests for explanations of human behavior.

One of the oldest theories, as I call it, is the "Four Personality Styles" behavioral theory. It first appeared as the Astrological Elements (Fire - Air - Earth - Water). Next came Exekiel's model (Bold - Far-seeing - Sturdy - Human) and then Empedocles (Hot - Dry - Cold - Wet).

In about 400 BC, Hippocrates created the most famous of these ancient models of human behavior, "The Four Temperaments" (Choleric - Sanguine - Phlegmatic - Melancholic). With it, he determined that human health and behaviors were influenced by the physical symptoms of blood, phlegm, and bile.

Variations came from Plato (Artistic - Intuitive - Reasoning - Sensible), Aristotle (Artistic - Intuitive - Logical - Care-Taking), Galen (Quick Tempered - Buoyant - Sluggish - Dejected), and Paracelsus (Passionate - Impulsive - Industrious - Calm). From that time until now, psychiatrists, psychologists, authors, teachers, behavioral experts, philosophers, business consultants, and others have implemented variations of this theory with millions of people.

The major breakthrough for the Four Personality Styles came in 1921, when Dr. Carl Jung divided people into his

"Four Archetypes"

Sensor - Intuitor - Thinker - Feeler

Building on Dr. Jung's work, dozens of contemporary models have separated people into these same four groupings. Examples include Myers-Briggs' Type Indicator, Personna Matrix System, D.I.S.C., Ned Hermann's Brain Dominance Instrument, Wilson Learning, and the Japanese Blood-Type Personality System. The "Appendix" (Page 206) has an extensive list of 190 variations of the "Four Personality Styles" behavioral theory.

Each variation of Four Personality Style theory generally advances only one of two potential benefits. Some promote an increased personal effectiveness by learning and improving one's own style, while others teach how to recognize and work with the styles of others.

Of all of these systems, only Galen's "Four Humors" truly departed from the practice of trying to define all people by four specific personalities. His was a system to cure disease, based on a therapy of opposites (sound familiar?).

However effective, none of these systems (excepting Galen's) have addressed the two inherent problems with all variations of the Four Personality Styles Behavioral Theory ... until now.

The Problem With Learning Your Own Style

The stated benefit of learning your personality style is; you are able to build on your strengths, while at the same time increasing your ability to predict your own negative behaviors. With this information, you will be able to make more effective choices.

While true, there can be a negative side effect to these systems. Instead of changing, people have been known to use this information to justify their own negative and non-productive behaviors. I have heard comments such as, *"It's my personality style to be direct. It's your problem if you can't handle it."*

The Turtle and the Scorpion

Once upon a time a scorpion asked a turtle to give him a ride across a stream. The turtle refused saying, *"I'll get you to the middle of the stream and you will sting me and I'll die."*

The scorpion replied, *"First, you have to realize there is no way I'd sting you. If I killed you, then I would surely drown. Second, it is quite possible that someday you might need a powerful friend, and I would owe you one."*

This made sense to the turtle. Since he always believed it was better to make a friend than an enemy, he decided to give the scorpion a ride.

The scorpion climbed on the back of the turtle's shell and they entered the water. Everything went fine until the turtle felt a pain on his neck. Sure enough, the scorpion had stung him.

As the turtle became paralyzed and started to drown, he managed to ask the now drowning scorpion why he had stung him. The scorpion replied, *"I couldn't help myself. It's my nature."*

186

The Problem With Categorizing the Styles of Others

Individuals and organizations have proved the benefits from these systems the world over for decades. Those armed with the knowledge of the four styles have found they could "usually" communicate more effectively with others.

Salespeople, in particular, have enjoyed the benefits of easier sales by targeting their sales approach to the specific styles of their clients and prospects. Another effective usage has been to fit prospective employees to specific jobs, by matching them with the appropriate style. For example: an "Analyzing" accountant, a "Promoting" sales manager, a "Supporting" assistant, or a "Controlling" plant manager (the style names are from the Integro-Persona Matrix system).

> **The problem?**
>
> **Nobody acts the same way all of the time.**

In the short term, there are definite advantages to both the organization and to the new employee. Unfortunately, when someone is reacting "out" of their normal style, and you are pre-disposed to treat them in one way, you will treat them exactly wrong ... on purpose.

Additionally, when circumstances change and you do not allow for the other person to be flexible enough to "grow" it can cause problems. One such example appears when there is an opportunity for advancement. People are often overlooked for promotion to a position for which they are qualified, because they are not viewed as possessing the "appropriate" characteristics.

As a result of such stereotyping people get cubby-holed. Management then spends time, money and effort to hire and train someone from the outside. This costs the organization even more when it loses a valuable, but frustrated, employee.

The Unique Advantage of "Four E's of Excellence"

By studying several different systems, including my own People Wheel, and the interactions of the participants, I have become aware of the advantages and disadvantages of all adaptations of the "Four Personality Styles" Behavioral Theory. More importantly, as previously stated, I have observed an important problem inherent to them all (except for Galen): All people behave according to their primary style most of the time. Nevertheless, nobody acts the same way all of the time, especially when they feel threatened.

The Four E's of Excellence system is based upon your being aware of your own current reactions, and not on your normal behavior or personality style. Love-based leadership results from changing your behaviors when stressed, instead of trying to control, manipulate, ignore, or pacify people with the intent to get them to change.

Interestingly, each fear-based reaction is just one of the Four E's of Excellence, but without its balancing opposite. Once you understand this, the solution becomes simple. When experiencing a fear-based reaction, do not deny it or let it overwhelm you, simply ADD its balancing opposite. Then, you remain in control of yourself.

BALANCING OPPOSITES

The **FIGHT** reaction is **Ethics without Empathy**,
so calm down and ADD EMPATHY

The **FLIGHT** reaction is **Enthusiasm without Evaluation**,
so slow down and ADD EVALUATION

The **FREEZE** reaction is **Evaluation without Enthusiasm**,
so lighten up and ADD ENTHUSIASM

The **FACADE** reaction is **Empathy without Ethics**,
so get real and ADD ETHICS

Therefore, when experiencing a fear-based reaction (Fight, Flight, Freeze, or Facade), you have a choice. Stop, breathe, and make the conscious choice to add the appropriate balancing opposite (Empathy, Evaluation, Enthusiasm, or Ethics), as each case requires, or continue with a behavior that you know would not work if someone were doing it to you.

If you choose to overcome your fear-based reactions in such a manner, your resulting love-based leadership will lead you to create personal and professional excellence. Regardless of your issues and circumstances, in times of stress or challenge, you always have a choice: Living fear-based or leading love-based. Choose wisely.

The Love-Based Leader TARGET ZONE

If you are not moving towards the center from love, then you are automatically moving to the extremes from fear. To overcome your negative fear-based reaction, and thus prevent the extreme fear-based reactions, strive to create the positive characteristic from the opposite inner quadrant.

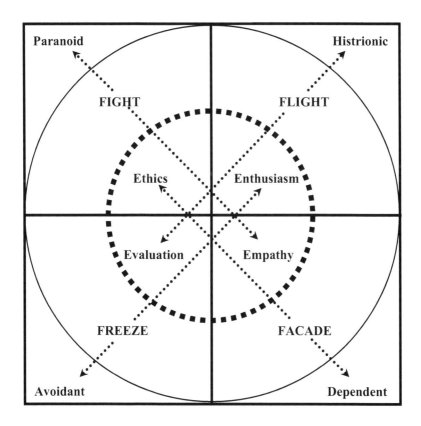

Balance is the Key

Stay in the Target Zone
(The Inner Circle)

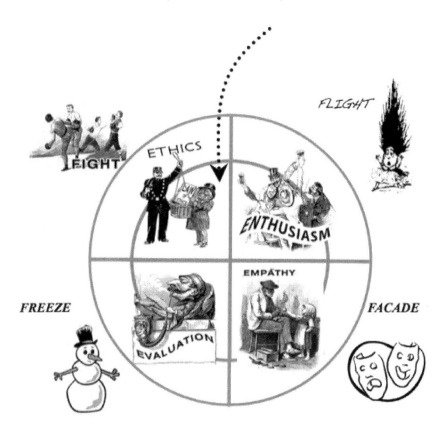

Summary – Using "Four E's of Excellence" on Yourself

When You ...	FIGHT	FLIGHT	FREEZE	FACADE
You Are TOO FOCUSED on:	Results	Relationships	Tasks & Commitments	Emotions & Feelings
You Tend to Ask:	**What?**	**Who?** or **When?**	**How?**	**Why?**
You Appear to Others to Be:	Aggressive Arrogant Critical Demanding Sarcastic	Distracted Harried Hurried Hyperactive Scattered	Anxious Inward Isolated Serious Withdrawn	Defensive Insecure Intimidated Phony Subordinate
Your Fear MANIFESTS as:	Judgmental	Frantic	Overwhelmed	Worried
You Are AT RISK of Becoming:	PARANOID	HISTRIONIC	AVOIDANT	DEPENDENT
You Solution is to ADD:	EMPATHY	EVALUATION	ENTHUSIASM	ETHICS
You Need to FOCUS on::	Emotions & Feelings	Tasks & Commitments	Time For Relationships	Results
You Need to Ask:	WHY?	HOW?	WHO or WHEN?	WHAT?
You Need to BECOME:	Accepting Compassionate Kind Nurturing Responsive	Deliberate Diligent Integral Patient Reliable	Creative Expressive Open Positive Promoting	Accountable Congruent Decisive Honest Thorough
Use This *Love-Based* TOOL:	The Trust Formula	Centering	Planned Spontaneity	Creating Desired Results
Your KEY is To:	FORGIVE	SLOW DOWN	PLAY	RISK
You Need to GIVE Others:	Courtesy	Details	Attention	Assurances
You Need To LET OTHERS:	Give To You	Speak	"In"	Know The Truth

191

EXERCISE #10 - Your Love-Based Leadership Qualities

Review the following four lists of attitudes, qualities, attributes, and behaviors. Circle each one that you feel you possess. Star (*) those that you have been able to demonstrate even when stressed. The challenge here is to be honest with yourself.

Characteristics of Love-Based Leadership

List A	List B	List C	List D
Accountable	Creative	Deliberate	Accepting
Bold	Energetic	Detailed	Accommodating
Confident	Enthusiastic	Diligent	Compassionate
Congruent	Exciting	Evaluative	Cooperative
Decisive	Expressive	Industrious	Courteous
Determined	Open	Integral	Empathetic
Ethical	Persuasive	Methodical	Friendly
Efficient	Positive	Patient	Kind
Focused	Promoting	Persistent	Nurturing
Honest	Spontaneous	Precise	Responsive
Thorough	Stimulating	Reliable	Supportive

Total the number of circled and starred items in each column:

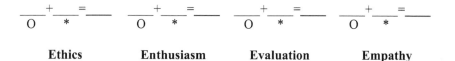

| Ethics | Enthusiasm | Evaluation | Empathy |

192

EXERCISE #10 - Continued

Your *Love-Based Leadership* Qualities

The List With Your **Highest** Number: _____
This is your PRIMARY *Love-Based Leadership* quality:

The List With Your **Next Highest** Number: _____
This is your SECONDARY *Love-Based Leadership* quality:

The List With Your **Next Highest** Number: _____
This is your UNCOMMON *Love-Based Leadership* quality:

The List With Your **Lowest** Number: _____
This is your RAREST *Love-Based Leadership* quality:

Hints:

If you always say what you mean and it's, *"Damn the torpedoes, full speed ahead"** when faced with difficulties or challenges, your primary quality is probably ETHICS. Your least demonstrated is most likely EMPATHY ... and you are certain of this.

If you feel that you demonstrate all four qualities equally, your primary quality is probably ENTHUSIASM. Your least demonstrated is most likely EVALUATION. You will resist this, but you need to look deeper.

If you analyze this for more than a minute, and/or do not feel you are very strong with any of them, your primary quality is probably EVALUATION, and your least demonstrated is most likely ENTHUSIASM.

If you worry about what others might think of your choices, your primary quality is probably EMPATHY, and your least demonstrated is most likely ETHICS (which you almost certainly will deny, but you probably will admit to telling white-lies).

* - Admiral Farragut, 1864

193

But What if "Four E's of Excellence" Does Not Work?

After you have examined and changed your behavior, if the person you are trying to reach is still not responding, only then does it make sense to evaluate their behavior. While most "Four Personality Style" systems are helpful for this, their effectiveness is greatly diminished when the self-evaluation step is glossed-over or skipped.

The best way to accomplish this is to remember the old axiom, *"When in Rome, do as the Romans do."* In other words, learn to speak the language of those who are reacting. In the case of Four E's of Excellence, that means:

If The Person You Are Trying To Reach is Reacting From:	Your Solution is to Lead With Love From:
FIGHT	**ETHICS**
FLIGHT	**ENTHUSIASM**
FREEZE	**EVALUATION**
FACADE	**EMPATHY**

On the following page, there are more specific suggestions. This is obviously only the tip of the iceberg. Nevertheless, with practice you will find it quite effective in assisting you in your quest to create desired results with love-based leadership, but only after looking at and changing yourself. *The Love-Based Leader, Book II* will deal with this tool in depth.

IMPORTANT:

Do NOT Try to Change Someone Else.

Again, Change Yourself.

Summary – Using "Four E's of Excellence" on OTHERS

When They ...	FIGHT	FLIGHT	FREEZE	FAÇADE
They Are TOO FOCUSED on:	Results	Relationships	Tasks & Commitments	Emotions & Feelings
They Tend to ASK:	**What?**	**Who? or When?**	**How?**	**Why?**
They Appear to You to Be:	Aggressive Arrogant Critical Demanding Sarcastic	Distracted Harried Hurried Hyperactive Scattered	Anxious Inward Isolated Serious Withdrawn	Defensive Insecure Intimidated Phony Subordinate
Their Fear MANIFESTS as::	Judgmental	Frantic	Overwhelmed	Worried
They Are AT RISK of Becoming:	PARANOID	HISTRIONIC	AVOIDANT	DEPENDENT
YOUR Solution is For YOU to ADD:	**ETHICS**	**ENTHUSIASM**	**EVALUATION**	**EMPATHY**
You Need to FOCUS on:	Results	Time For Relationships	Tasks & Commitments	Emotions & Feelings
You Need to ASK:	**WHAT?**	**WHO or WHEN?**	**HOW?**	**WHY?**
YOU Need to BECOME:	Accountable Congruent Decisive Honest Thorough	Creative Expressive Open Positive Promoting	Deliberate Diligent Integral Patient Reliable	Accepting Compassionate Kind Nurturing Responsive
Use This *Love-Based* TOOL:	Creating Desired Results	Planned Spontaneity	Centering	The Trust Formula
You KEY is to:	**RISK**	**PLAY**	**SLOW DOWN**	**FORGIVE**
You Need to GIVE Them:	Assurances	Attention	Details	Courtesy
You Need To LET THEM:	**Know The Truth**	**"In"**	**SPEAK**	**Give To You**

The Global Love-Based Leader

Over the last 30 years, there has been a global shift in leadership effectiveness. Managers, executives, parents, spouses, teachers, community leaders, elected officials, and other position-power fear-based reactors are increasingly frustrated because the old "solutions" are simply not working anymore.

Sometimes the problems are so overwhelming it can be easy to demonstrate one or more of the four fear-based reactions. However, whether it is Fight, Flight, Freeze, or Facade, the one certainty is that when you are reacting, you become part of the problem ... because it gives others an excuse to react to you.

There are times when something so devastating occurs, you cry out for someone to take action. However, when you feel a fire in your belly about the "wrongness" of an incident, and all you do is react, you have bastardized your own integrity. At that moment you have the chance to become part of the solution, but only if you choose to lead with love.

"We are not going to be able to operate our Spaceship Earth

successfully, nor for much longer,

unless we see it as a whole spaceship and our fate as common.

It has to be everybody or nobody."

R. Buckminster Fuller

Worldwide, we are desperately in need of leaders: Not position-power fear-based reactors, but global love-based leaders. Fear makes a poor foundation for the choice of "right" and "wrong". The only chance for peace to prevail is through the practice of the love-based qualities of Ethics, Enthusiasm, Evaluation, and Empathy.

To many, the concept of love-based leadership sounds like pleasant philosophy. The perception is that anyone who strives to live up to this ideal will be walked-on in relationships, taken advantage of in business, and ridiculed or resisted (or worse) on the global stage.

Global love-based leaders such as Jesus Christ, Mother Teresa, Abraham Lincoln, St. Francis of Assisi, Buckminster Fuller, Dr. Martin Luther King, Jr., Dr. Albert Schweitzer, Mahatma Gandhi, Nelson Mandela and others have demonstrated the powerful alternative of love-based leadership. We have studied, honored, praised, and even worshiped the few who have lived this truth, but rarely have we made honest efforts to emulate them.

There are two reasons for this. First, the very effectiveness of such distinguished lives seems to elevate each of these "saints" to a higher stature above us "normal" people. Indeed, it almost feels arrogant to imagine being able to accomplish results in such a love-based manner.

Second, these people have always paid a penalty for their successes. They have often toiled alone against seemingly impossible odds. They have been criticized and ridiculed. Many have been imprisoned or attacked, and some have even been killed. These prices, or even the possibility of them, are too high for most people to consider.

Position-power fear-based reactors generally view love-based solutions as naive, ineffective, foolhardy, and even dangerous. As a result, fear-based reactions abound. *"I don't get mad I get even.";* *"I don't have to take this, I'm out of here.";* *"If you can't say something nice, don't say anything at all.";* and *"Don't Rock the Boat,"* have become their mantras.

Yes, there is a risk in choosing love-based leadership. However, there is a greater risk for failing to do so. The time has come to take the "saints" off their pedestals. It is an insult to honor these people, while refusing to walk in their footsteps.

We can no longer afford the luxury of leaving

Love-Based Leadership **in the hands of the very few.**

Most people have learned how to fight against something, but few have learned how to fight for something ... especially when threatened. Some people are gung-ho to fight terrorists, while others are attacking the people who support war. "Peace-Nicks" and "War-Mongers", as they unaffectionately label each other, have one thing in common ... they are both fear-based in their attacks on each other.

What effects are fear-based reactions having on Post-9/11 America, and the rest of the world? Is the movement more towards Oneness or Separation? Acceptance or Judgment? Love or Hate? Peace or War?

The concept of *Love-Based Leadership* is not new.
You have heard it all many times, and in many ways:

- - - - - - - - - - - - - - - - -

"Do unto others as you would have them do unto you."
"The Golden Rule." Jesus, The Holy Bible, Matthew 7:12

*"Not one of you truly believes until you wish for others
what you wish for yourself."*
Islam – The Prophet Muhammad, Hadith

"When you hurt someone else, you hurt yourself even more."
Your Grandmother

"What is hateful to you, do not do to your neighbor."
Judaism – Hillel, Talmud, Shabbat 31a

"Treat not others in ways that you yourself would find hurtful."
Buddhism – The Buddha, Udana-Varga 5.18

*"For every action there is an equal and opposite reaction,
and a resultant."*
Sir Isaac Newton

"Do not do to others what would cause pain if done to you."
Hinduism – Mahabharata 5:1517

"Do not do to others what you do not want done to yourself."
Confucianism – Confucius, Analects 15:23

> *"We are but strands in the web of life.*
> *Whatsoever we do to the web, we do to ourselves."*
> Chief Seattle, of the Suquamish and
> Duwamish Native American Tribes

> *"Lay not on any soul a load that you would not wish to be*
> *laid upon you, and desire not for anyone the things*
> *you would not desire for yourself."*
> Baha'I Faith – Baha'u'llah, Gleanings

> *"And in the end, the love you take is equal to the love you make."*
> *The End, Abbey Road* – The Beatles, Lennon & McCartney

> Finally, I contribute:
> *And in the end, the hate you take is equal to the hate you make.*

If you think these equations are wrong, then you need to look deeper. Whatever the questions may be, fear-based reactions triggered by resentment, judgment, prejudice, and hate, are not the answers.

Yes, love-based leadership can sound naive. Let's face it, *"All You Need Is Love"* is easy only when everyone else is being loving. Nevertheless, I challenge you to overcome your fear-based reactions and create personal and professional greatness as a love-based leader.

Love-based leaders are needed in families that are being decimated by fear-based reactions. There is an urgent need for corporate love-based leaders, as the greed of executives in companies such as Enron, WorldCom, Arthur Anderson, Countrywide, Lehman Brothers, Goldman Sachs, and AIG have produced an increasingly fear-based economy.

Love-based leaders are needed in government, as fear-based and bitterly divided politicians cannot possibly accomplish the business of the people. There is a desperate need for global love-based leaders, as all acts of terrorism and the reactions to those acts are fear-based.

When taken all together, there is an unprecedented need for love-based leaders. It is important to note that while love-based leaders do not react when threatened, they are not pacifists. Mother Teresa was a warrior. However, she fought her battles with love.

A Sense of Urgency

Throughout history there have been those who became love-based leaders in spite of great obstacles, and who continued to affect the lives of others long after their deaths. Perhaps you have known a love-based leader who, while not famous, inspired you in some manner before he or she passed away ... a friend, relative, teacher, or business mentor.

All of these people had something in common with one another, and eventually with you and me ... life is simply not long enough. There is never enough time.

My son Shaunessy was born 6 ½ weeks premature. He was so small and fragile we had to leave him in the hospital for several weeks. When we were finally allowed to take him home, I remember my mother holding him in her hands (and she has small hands). She looked up at me with a tear in her eye and said, *"This was you, just a heartbeat ago."* Just another heartbeat later, he is 24 and working in Hollywood and already has his first movie credit (The Informant).

There are no guarantees in life. Whether you only survive another five minutes or live a hundred more years, the only valid question is, *"What are you going to do with the time you have left?"*

Fear-Based Living is becoming a thing of the past.

Position-Power Fear-Based Leaders are history.

Love-Based Leadership is the way of the Future.

If you truly wish to make a greater impact with your life than you ever imagined, then the path of love-based leadership will empower you to manifest your dreams. Someday, when you have achieved excellence in all areas of your life, it will not matter to you if anyone else knows. You will know. With this knowledge, you will be filled with peace when you look back on your life, because you will be proud of what you did with it.

Time passes so quickly. Cherish each day by living with a sense of urgency. **Nevertheless, there is another reason you need a sense of urgency. It is huge.**

The Love-Based Leadership Boom

The world changed in 1976. There is now enough of everything for everyone. Buckminster Fuller calculated that we are doing so much more with so much less that not only should nobody be starving, every human on "Spaceship Earth" could be living as billionaires.

All children born after 1976 (and perhaps even those born a bit before that) are unique in history. Whether they consciously realize it or not, they are experiencing the world from the "enough for everyone" perspective.

Nevertheless, they have been raised by well-meaning pre-1976 parents, with a "not enough for everyone" consciousness. These children need love-based leaders to be their mentors. This is critical, because the children that they will raise will be the most powerful generation of love-based leaders the world has ever seen.

It will be their children who will represent another "Baby Boom". Not the population boom of Post World War II, but the "Love-Based Leadership Boom" of children born of post-1976 parents. It will be a global revolution far more profound than the 1960's.

These are, and will be, the first people to have been raised by parents who according to Buckminster Fuller, were born in a world where there is enough of everything for everyone. They will come to see that the only obstacle for world peace is the mindset of their well-meaning fear-based elders.

There is a large and growing population of young people striving to become love-based leaders. As such, they will not respond to fear-based parenting, fear-based educating, fear-based advertising, or fear-based political campaigning in the same ways as their parents and grandparents.

The World has enough people living fear-based. We need love-based leaders and we need them now. They are needed to pave the way for the first generation of potential love-based leaders who should be making their presence felt about 2020.

The shift of human consciousness is near. The "Love-Based Leadership Boom" will occur with you or without you. It will be quicker with you. Now is the time to teach the concepts of love-based leadership by putting them into action. Do it now.

Regardless of your circumstances, and how you feel about them, you really do have a choice ...

Live Fear-Based – or – *Lead Love-Based*

The Children Are Watching.

JAMES ROSWELL QUINN

James Roswell "Ross" Quinn is an international keynote speaker, author, leadership trainer, success coach, and CFE Certified Financial Educator®. Since 1972, he has presented over 1,500 keynote addresses, corporate workshops, personal growth workshops, relationship retreats, and leadership trainings to tens of thousands of people in the USA, Canada, Panama, Dubai, New Zealand, Thailand, Mexico, Bahamas, and Dominican Republic. He has coined the phrases, "Love-Based Leader", "Fear-Based Reactor", "Impersonal Power", "Victimary" (as opposed to Visionary), "Pre-Actions", and "Get Over Yourself".

Quinn's corporate seminars and keynote addresses (Speaking Of Success, Get Over Yourself, The People Wheel, and Four E's of Excellence) have been presented to dozens of businesses and organizations worldwide. Participants learn how to lead and communicate more effectively, in order to create a more positive work environment, reduce conflict, improve customer service, develop faster time-to-market, and reduce employee turnover.

Quinn Client List

Walt Disney Feature Animation

Microtel ... Kodak ... Mitsubishi ... Van de Kamp's

Nightingale-Conant Corporation

State Farm Insurance ... Lincoln National Life ... Pacific Mutual Life

Materiel Management Institute of Canada

Cornell University ... Rochester Institute of Technology ... Tech de Monterrey

Real Property Institute of Canada

Nolan Real Estate Services ... Video Law ... Institutional Financial Services

ReMax Realty (USA, Canada and New Zealand)

Auckland Multiple Listing Bureau ... Toronto Real Estate Board

Six Chicago-Area Banks

NAV CANADA ... K Walsh Travel (Toronto) ... CANDYM

Seven Multi-Level Marketing (MLM) companies

... and many others.

James Roswell Quinn is on a quest to provide people with the tools to attain and maintain excellence in their professional and personal relationships. He published the first version of this book, *Controlling Others For Love And Profit*, in 2004. Ross followed this with his 8-CD Personal Audio Seminar entitled, "**Get Over Yourself**," in 2006. Next, in 2007, Quinn co-authored the self-help book *Speaking Of Success* with Ken Blanchard (*The One Minute Manager*), Jack Canfield (*Chicken Soup For The Soul*), and Stephen R. Covey (*The 7 Habits of Highly Effective People*).

In September 2007, Quinn was a featured speaker at the Toronto Expo Centre for the world's first convention for the best-selling book and DVD, The Secret. Although he was not a contributor to the book or the DVD, his presentation, "**The Secret of the Secret**", had the largest and most enthusiastic audience of the conference.

Ross and his wife Christine developed their **Conscious Couples** weekend to help people create more effective and committed intimate relationships. Its premise is that troubled couples need joy, not work.

In 2010, James Roswell Quinn was accepted into the non-profit Heartland Institute of Financial Education as a **CFE Certified Financial Educator®**. The Heartland Institute, in conjunction with colleges and universities, provides nation-wide education courses to help workers better manage their personal finances and company benefits, thus allowing companies to satisfy their fiduciary responsibilities as laid out in the Pension Protection Act.

For over three decades, Quinn has inspired participants from around the world to make greater contributions WITH their lives. His **Global Impact Leadership Retreat** utilizes rock climbing, high ropes "confidence" courses, Tai Chi "Quinn", studies of Mother Teresa and Buckminster Fuller, as well as indoor and outdoor group activities. Everything in this unique and powerful course is designed to assist people in increasing their leadership skills and inter-personal effectiveness.

When Quinn runs his **New Zealand Global Impact Leadership Retreat**, he combines it with an Adventure Tour where he adds bungee jumping, white-water rafting, boat tours, thermal-area walks, hiking on glaciers, jet-boating, wine tastings, black-water rafting (through underground caves), swimming with dolphins, and touring Hobbiton and other *Lord of the Rings* film sites.

Whether in a book, CD, keynote address, financial literacy workshop, leadership training, success coaching, personal growth seminar, or adventure trip, Quinn's leading-edge human development technology empowers love-based leaders to create desired results by overcoming their fear-based reactions. As a result, many thousands of people worldwide have created greater successes in their personal and professional lives than they had ever dreamed possible.

James Roswell Quinn was born in Seattle, Washington in 1950. He grew up in the Los Angeles area and graduated from the University of Southern California in 1972, with a B.S. in Business Administration.

Quinn is the father of six children. He and Christine make their home in Lake Summerset, Illinois.

ACKNOWLEDGEMENTS

All of the following people have contributed to *The Love-Based Leader*. Without their stories, editing, feedback, financial backing, love, and encouragement this book simply would not exist.

Thank you German Avila, Karen Barnes, Jennifer Kaia Bartok, Janet Battaglio, Rudy Bazelmans, Regina Blake, Ross & Annette Bradbury, David Bryan, Darlene Buckingham, Paul Camp, Emily Cieslinski, Rob Cleverly, Angie Coleman, Jose Colon, Peter Comrie, Nancy & Jim Cooper, Diane Costello, Jackie Cowan, Linda Cowan, Paul & Nancy Cushman, Danny Dehm, Aida Dennehy, Fred & Beth Dewey, Lina DiSanto, Wade Domet, Mark Doyle, Tom & Shirley Dusmet, The Dusmet Family, Josie & Alan Estill, Karen Evans, JoAnne & Sam Feil, Kate & Michael Ferguson, Cally Field, Bobby Fielding, Marlene & Charlie Fisher, Dave Gant, Beverly & Bill Gleason, Danielle Gleason, Adelaide Gomer, David Good, Roger & Jackie Grey-Moores, Steve Guizzetti, Guy & Nan Hanna-Paquin, Michell Hays, Greg Heaney, Barbara Hellman, Cindy Hoy, Craig & Barbara Imrie, Anne James, Lee Jeavons, Jillian Jeffery, Phil & Brenda Johnson, Kathy Jones, George Kaufman, Lila Keller, Shannon Kelly, Faye Kendel, Andre Kennedy, Kathleen & Jon Kores, Rebecca Kraai, Brenda Lawrie, Irv & Dorothy Lesch, Sharon Lilla, Syl Leduc, Fernanda Avila & Roberto Martinez, Amy May, Nancy May, Jan McCormick, Gaël Messoah, Tim & Patty Michels, David Mock, Rena Gaile & James Morgan, John Nemanic, Jackie Perry, Robert Peshka, Sandra Pierce, Michael Pinkney, Dennis Ponczkowski, Patricia Price, Josef & Jenny Puehringer, Gary & Cynthia Quinn, Maureen Rieckhof, Gail Robertson, the Rochester Agape Club, Patrick Salimi, Jan & Bob Sanders, Richard and Carolyn Santee, Barbara Sarratori, Joan Simnett, Stephen Smith, Norma & David Spall, Mary & Alan Temple, Toronto IPI #77, Steve Tucker, Janice Tuschong, Elaine Vanier, Roddy Vanier, Gary Van Camp, Lew VonAlmen, John Wagner, Kimberly Walsh, George & Susan Buckley-Watson, Elaine Webster, Dr. Greg Weathers, Chris & Sue Weiss, Gabrielle Weiss, Paula Wemp, J. R. Wheelwright, Mike & Char Wood, Carol Yacono, Anita & Steve Yoder, Pastor William Yonker (Immanuel Lutheran Church), Todd Zdanowski, and one person who prefers to remain anonymous.

To Brandi Jasmine – my editor and webmaster: All I can say is how much gratitude I have for how good you have made me look, and for how patient you have been. This book will reach more people because of you. Many other people assisted with the editing of the seemingly endless re-writes. But I want to say a special thank you to the efforts of Nan Hanna-Paquin, Bob Sanders, Steve Tucker, Bobby Fielding, Aida Dennehy, Cindy Hoy, and Fred Dewey.

To Christine Quinn – my wife and business partner: Your co-writing was brilliant. You have a special way of helping me communicate my actual intent, with clarity. No matter how many times I asked you to read something, you always managed to see my work through the eyes of new readers and help me find a better way to express my ideas.

To Steven Sieden: I cannot express to you how deeply I appreciate your Foreword to this book. The first time I read it, I felt as if Buckminster Fuller himself was introducing me through you. You are a gifted writer and I am humbled to have your support.

To Peter Fromme-Douglas: Thank you for the wonderful photograph and many illustrations. Your abilities as an artist are rare gifts, but I will always remember the afternoon we came up with the original outrageous title, *Controlling Others For Love And Profit*. Oh, how hard we laughed.

To Janet Eve Sanders – my mother: I need to say how profoundly you have affected my life. Your living example taught me of love-based leadership long before I learned the term. No "thank you" can be enough, but thank you.

To James Holden Quinn – my father: Your footprints can be found on almost every page of this book. You were my mentor, my business partner, and my friend – and I miss you.

Finally, I thank all of the people whom I have taught, coached, or advised. You have come from many experiences, backgrounds, cultures, and nationalities. You have taught me far more than I could possibly have taught you. Because of you, I have learned that while it is our unique differences that make life interesting, it is our similarities that bring us together.

The world has enough people living fear-based. We need more love-based leaders. We need you, and we need you now.

Thank you,

"Ross"
James Roswell Quinn

"Never doubt that a small group of committed citizens can change the world.

Indeed, it is the only thing that ever has."

Margret Mead

APPENDIX
Variations of the *"Four Personality Styles"*

As previously stated in Chapter 10, one of the oldest behavioral theories, as I call it, is the *"Four Personality Styles"*. It first appeared as the **Astrological Elements** (Fire - Air - Earth - Water).

Later came **Hippocrates" Four Temperaments**
(Choleric - Sanguine - Melancholic - Phlegmatic)

Then came **Dr. Carl Jung's Four Archetypes**
(Intuitor - Sensor - Thinker - Feeler)

Which paved the way for the **Myers-Briggs Type Indicator**
(Intuition - Sensates - Thinkers - Feelers)

Following are 190 models (plus 55 examples from history, TV, books, and movies) that are in some way reflective of, or based upon, the Four Personality Styles behavioral theory. Some of these systems focus on self-awareness and self-improvement, but most are focused on the understanding, categorizing, management, control, motivation, or improvement of others.

Interestingly, only Galen's system of curing disease with his *"Therapy of Opposites"* is similar in usage to Four E's of Excellence, which shows people how to overcome fear-based reactions with their opposite love-based solutions.

I began compiling this data in 1975, simply because my first exposure to Four Personality Styles systems intrigued me. I doubt that you could find a more comprehensive list.

While this is an extensive list, there are bound to be errors and omissions and my interpretations are certainly open to debate. This collection is presented here to show the widespread application of the Four Personality Styles behavioral theory, and the similarities between the different variations. Regardless of the manner in which each system interprets or utilizes the theory, you will notice how the labels and patterns of the "Four Personality Styles" generally remain consistent and synonymous.

For ease of comparison, these *Four Personality Style* systems
are grouped into the following "**Typical Orientations**":

Style 1	Style 2	Style 3	Style 4
Results	Relationships	Tasks	Feelings & Emotions

Historic "Four Personality Styles" Models

Typical Orientation	Style 1 Results	Style 2 Relationships	Style 3 Tasks	Style 4 Feelings & Emotions
ASTROLOGY The Four Elements	THE FIRE SIGNS Aires Leo Sagittarius	THE AIR SIGNS Gemini Libra Aquarius	THE EARTH SIGNS Taurus Virgo Capricorn	THE WATER SIGNS Cancer Scorpio Pisces
CHINESE ASTROLOGY The Four Animal Trines	THE FIRST TRINE Rat Dragon Monkey	THE THIRD TRINE Tiger Horse Dog	THE SECOND TRINE Ox Snake Rooster	THE FOURTH TRINE Rabbit Sheep Pig
Exekiel (590 BC)	Bold	Far-Seeing	Sturdy	Humane
Empedocles (450 BC) The Four Qualities	Hot – Zeus	Dry – Goea	Cold – Hera	Wet – Poseidon
Hippocrates (370 BC) Four Temperaments	Choleric ANGRY	Sanguine CHEERFUL	Melancholic SAD	Phlegmatic NEUTRAL
Plato (350 BC)	Intuitive	Artistic	Reasoning	Sensible
Aristotle (325 BC)	Noetic – Intuitive	Iconic – Artistic	Dianoetic – Logical	Pistic – Care Taking
Galen (150 AD) Four Body Humors	Quick-Tempered	Buoyant	Sluggish	Dejected
Irenaeus (185 AD) Four Temperaments	Spiritual	Spontaneous	Scholarly	Historical
Paracelsus (1550 AD) Four Totem Spirits	Nymphs PASSIONATE	Salamanders IMPULSIVE	Gnomes INDUSTRIOUS	Sylphs CALM
Hopi Medicine Wheel	Spirit	Body	Mind	Heart

Early 20th Century "Four Personality Styles" Models

Typical Orientation	Style 1 Results	Style 2 Relationships	Style 3 Tasks	Style 4 Feelings & Emotions
Eric Adickes (1907) Four World Views	Dogmatic	Innovative	Traditional	Agnostic
Adler (1920) 4 Mistaken Goals	Power	Revenge	Service	Recognition
Abraham Maslow (1920) Levels of Organization	Autocratic	Motivational	Custodial	Collegial
Ernst Kretschmer (1920)	Insensitive	Manic	Depressive	Oversensitive
Dr. Carl Jung (1921) The Four Archetypes	Intuitor	Sensor	Thinker	Feeler
Edward Spanger (1928) Four Human Values	Religious	Artistic	Economic	Theoretic
William Marston (1928) *Emotions of Normal People*	Dominance	Inducement	Steadiness	Compliance
Myers-Briggs (1942) MBTI Myers-Briggs Type Indicator	Intuition	Sensates	Thinkers	Feelers
Eric Fromm (1947)	Exploitative	Marketing	Hoarding	Receptive
Luft & Ingham (1950) The Johari Window	Blind	Open	Unknown	Hidden
Hans Eysenck (1955) Trait Examples	Restless	Outgoing	Reliable	Reserved
Myers (1958)	Tough-Minded	Probing	Scheduling	Friendly

Some Basic "Four Personality Styles" Models

Typical Orientation	Style 1 Results	Style 2 Relationships	Style 3 Tasks	Style 4 Feelings & Emotions
John Geier – DiSC	Dominance	Influence	Steadiness	Compliance
Sandler Sales Institute	Dominant	Influencer	Steady Relater	Compliant
McQuaig Institute **Selling Styles**	Dominance	Sociability	Relaxation	Compliance
Performance Trainers	Dominant	Extrovert	Patient	Conformist
D.E.S.A.	Dominant	Expressive	Analytical	Solid
The Four S's	Self-Propelled	Spirited	Systematic	Solid
Fred Pryor **CareerTrack**	Director	**Socializer**	**Thinker**	**Relater**
Cathcart & Alessandra **Relationship Strategies**	Director	Socializer	Thinker	Relater
Michael Lovas **About People**	Commander	Expressive	Thinker	Nurturer
L.I.F.O.	Directing	Doing	Planning	Inspiring
What's My Style?	Direct	Spirited	Systematic	Considerate

More "Four Personality Styles" Models

Typical Orientation	Style 1 Results	Style 2 Relationships	Style 3 Tasks	Style 4 Feelings & Emotions
McCarter **Teamwork Styles**	Driver Traditionalist	Catalyst Expressive	Visionary Analytical	Amiable Troubleshooter
Wilson Learning	Driver	**Expressive**	**Analytic**	**Amiable**
Merrill & Reid **Personal Styles**	Driver	Expressive	Analytical	Amiable
D. Forbes Ley **The Best Seller**	Driver	Expressive	Analytical	Amiable
John William Wright **Communication Styles**	Driver	Expressive	Analytical	Amiable
Don Hutson **Social Styles**	Driver	Expressive	Analytical	Amiable
MMPI Minnesota Multiphasic Personality Inventory	Driver	Expressive	Analytical	Amiable
The Four A's	Administrative	Active	Analytical	Amiable
L.E.A.D.	Leader	Expressor	Dependable	Amiable
Spirit Totems **Animal Speak** Ted Andrews	**FIRE –** The Magic of **Creation**	**AIR –** The Magic of **Higher Vision & Prophecy**	**EARTH –** The Magic of **Manifestation**	**WATER –** The Magic of **Shapeshifting**

210

And More "Four Personality Styles" Models

Typical Orientation	Style 1 Results	Style 2 Relationships	Style 3 Tasks	Style 4 Feelings & Emotions
David Keirsey (1984) - *Please Understand Me*	Guardian	Artisan	Rationalist	Idealist
Linda Berens **Temperament Patterns**	Guardian	Artisan	Rational	Idealist
Personality Zone	Guardians	Artisans	Rationals	Idealists
Keirsey/Bates Four Temperaments	Epimethean **Dutiful**	Dionysian **Artful**	Promethean **Technological**	Apollonian **Soulful**
M. Wolfe AOL - Find A Job	The Guardian (or Duty Seeker)	The Artisan (or Action-Seeker)	The Analyzer	The Idealist
IPersonic	Realist	Doer	Analytical	Idealist
Integro Persona Matrix System	Controller	**Promoter**	**Analyzer**	**Supporter**
P.S.I.	Controller	Promoter	Analyst	Supporter
James H Quinn-- **P.E.P. People Effective People**	Controlling	Promoting	Analyzing	Supporting
Jard DeVille *Nice Guys Finish First*	Controller	Entertainer	Comprehender	Supporter
Stuart Atkins *Life Orientations*	Controlling-Taking	Adapting-Dealing	Conserving-Holding	Supporting-Giving
Toastmaster's **Four Personalities**	The Controller	The Star	The Quiet One	The Talker

Roles "Four Personality Styles" Models

Typical Orientation	Style 1 Results	Style 2 Relationships	Style 3 Tasks	Style 4 Feelings & Emotions
Robert Kiyosaki *Rich Dad Poor Dad* CASH FLOW Quadrant	B – Big-Business Owners	S – Small-Business Person or Self-Employed	I – Investor	E – Employee
Career Possibilities (High School – Career Aptitude Test)	Management Law Enforcement Attorney	Sales Entertainment Politics	Accounting Engineering Scientist	Human Resources Counseling Nursing
Sales Sense Kelly Burnette	Producer	Actor	Stage Hand	Director
Roger Hamilton	Star	Deal Maker	Mechanic	Accumulator
Robert Moore *Archetypes of the Mature Masculine*	King	Warrior	Magician	Lover
Cliff Barry Shadow Work	Sovereign	Warrior	Magician	Lover
George Sheehan *The Four Roles*	Saint	Animal	Craftsman	Friend
Facebook Personality Test	Judging Intuitive	Extraverted Feeling	Introverted Thinking	Perceiving Sensing
Irwin Thompson *Archetypes in History*	Leader	Hunter	Shaman	Fool
ImaginiVisualDNA	Conqueror	Thriller	Worker Bee	Escape Artist
Angeles Arrien *The Four Fold Way*	Visionary	Warrior	Teacher	Healer
Shannon Thunderbird	Visionary	Warrior	Teacher	Healer
Brownsword	Visionaries	Catalysts	Stabilizers	Negotiators
McCarter	Visionary	Catalyst	Traditionalist	Amiable

212

Relationship "Four Personality Styles" Models

Typical Orientation	Style 1 Results	Style 2 Relationships	Style 3 Tasks	Style 4 Feelings & Emotions
David Keirsey (1998) - Please Understand Me II	Helpmate	Playmate	Mindmate	Soulmate
Thomas Harris MD *I'm OK You're OK*	I'm OK – You're not OK	I'm OK – You're OK	I'm not OK – You're not OK	I'm not OK – You're OK
Robert Needlman **Bound by Birth Order**	First Born	Youngest Child	Only Child	Middle Child
DHarmony Advice	First Born	Youngest	Only Child	Second Born
Stephen C Lundin **FISH!**	Make Their Day	Play	Be There	Choose Your Attitude
The Four Elements of Trust **A.R.C.O.**	Congruent	Open	Reliable	Accepting
Human Synergistics Distinctive Circumplex	Satisfaction Orientation	People Orientation	Task Orientation	Security Orientation
Kirschner/Brinkman **Understanding Communication Styles**	Get It Done	Get Appreciated	Get It Right	Get Along
Japanese Blood-Type Personality System	Type O	Type AB	Type A	Type B
Wriths/Bowman-Kruhm	Organizing & Belonging	Acting & Impacting	Understanding & Knowing	Caring & Questioning
C.I.A. Personality Profile	**Impressive – Mastermind**	**Daring – Thrill Seeker**	**Thoughtful – Observer**	**Curious – Adventurer**
Theodore Millon	Ambivalent	Independent	Detached	Dependent
Len Sperry Effective Leadership	Self-Confident	Adventurous	Leisurely	Dramatic
Quinn Incorporated **The People Wheel**	**Congruent**	**Persuade**	**Deliberate**	**Accommodate**

213

Management "Four Personality Styles" Models

	Style 1 Results	Style 2 Relationships	Style 3 Tasks	Style 4 Feelings & Emotions
Typical Orientation				
B.E.S.T.	**Bold**	**Expressive**	**Technical**	**Sympathetic**
Spencer Johnson *Who Moved My Cheese?*	Hem	Scurry	Sniff	Haw
Type A or B	Type A – Motivated	Type A – Messy	Type B – Compulsive	Type B – Casual
Don Miguel Ruiz *The Four Agreements*	Be impeccable with your word	Don't take anything seriously	Don't make assumptions	Always do your best
Jairek Robbins	Results	Action	Beliefs	Potential
Eastman Kodak Motivational Styles	NIC Negative-Instantaneous Consequences	PIC Positive-Instantaneous Consequences	NUC Negative-Uncertain Consequences	PUC Positive-Uncertain Consequences
Linda Berens Interaction Styles	In-Charge	Get-Things-Going	Chart-the-Course	Behind-the-Scenes
Allen Fahden **4 Dominant Attributes**	Creator	Advancer	Refiner	Executor
L.I.N.K.	Know	Network	Learn	Interact
Richard Montgomery **People Patterns**	Says what is – Does what works	Says what's possible – Does what works	Says what is – Does what's right	Says what's possible – Does what's right
Cardinal Stories	Rational – Objective	Emotional – Objective	Rational – Subjective	Emotional – Subjective
Kalil (1998) *Follow Your True Colors to the Work You Love*	Courageous	Conceptual	Conventional	Compassionate
Kathy Kolbe **The Kolbe Index**	Follow-Through	Quick-Start	Fact-Finder	Implementor
Bruce Tuckman **Team Development**	Forming	Storming	Preforming	Norming

Organizational "Four Personality Styles" Models

Typical Orientation	Style 1 Results	Style 2 Relationships	Style 3 Tasks	Style 4 Feelings & Emotions
Dr. Ravi Batra *The Great Depression of 1990* (Types of Nations)	Acquisitors	Warriors	Intellectuals	Laborers
The Harvard Corporate Cultures Wall Street Journal 7/17/89	**Fortresses**	**Baseball Teams**	**Academies**	**Clubs**
Blake-Mouton **Managerial Grid**	Task Management	Team Management	Impoverished Management	Country Club Management
Ohio State University **Leadership Model**	High-Structure Low-Consideration	Low-Structure High-Consideration	High-Structure Low-Consideration	Low-Structure High-Consideration
Political Compass	Authoritarian - Right	Libertarian - Right	Authoritarian - Left	Libertarian- Left
Worlds Smallest Political Quiz	Statist Big Government	Right - Conservative	Left - Liberal	Libertarian
Harry Potter	**Slytherin**	**Gryffindor**	**Ravenclaw**	**Hufflepuff**
The Peace Pole	East (Japan)	West (USA)	North (Germany)	South (Russia)
Jonathan Knaupp **ARRAY**	Production	Connection	Harmony	Status Quo
United States of America Constitution	Executive Branch **The President**	Legislative Branch **The Congress**	Judicial Branch **The Supreme Court**	The Electorate *"We The People"*

215

Thinking & Learning "Four Personality Styles" Models

Typical Orientation	Style 1 Results	Style 2 Relationships	Style 3 Tasks	Style 4 Feelings & Emotions
Bandler & Grinder **Neuro-Linguistic Programming**	Visual	Kinesthetic	Digital	Auditory
Bernice McCarthy **About Learning**	Imaginative Learning	Dynamic Learning	Analytic Learning	Common Sense Learning
Honey & Mumford **Learning Styles**	Pragmatist	Activist	Theorist	Reflector
Keith Golay **Learning Types**	Conceptual - Specific	Actual - Spontaneous	Actual - Routine	Conceptual - Global
David Kolb **Learning Styles**	Converging	Diverging	Assimilating	Accommodating
Janet Rae-Dupree Learning Styles (NY Times 5/4/08)	Procedurally	Innovatively	Analytically	Relationally
Anthony Gregorc **Thinking Styles**	Abstract – Sequential	Abstract - Random	Concrete - Sequential	Concrete - Random
High School "Explore" **Standards Achievement**	Ideas & Things	People & Ideas	Data & Things	People & Data
Orientation Counseling	Prophetic	Intuitive	Visionary	Feeling
Katherine Benziger **Thinking Styles Assessment**	Frontal Left	Basal Left	Basal Right	Frontal Right
Conscious Competence **Learning Matrix**	Unconscious Competence	Unconscious Incompetence	Conscious Competence	Conscious Incompetence
Thomas Gordon **Learning Stages**	Unconsciously Skilled	Unconsciously Unskilled	Consciously Skilled	Consciously Unskilled
Ken Wilber **4 Quadrants Model**	Intersubjective Cultural	Interobjective Social	Subjective Introspective	Objective Behavioral
Richard Barrett **Vision & Mission Development**	Internal Vision	External Vision	Internal Mission	External Mission

216

Animal "Four Personality Styles" Models

Typical Orientation	Style 1 Results	Style 2 Relationships	Style 3 Tasks	Style 4 Feelings & Emotions
Exekiel – 590 BC	Lion	Eagle	Ox	Man
Jeffrey Combs The Animal Factor	Lion	Monkey	Owl	Koala
Gary Smalley Four Personalities	Lion	Otter	Beaver	Golden Retriever
Edward Horrell More Than Words	Lion	Fox	Koala	Porpoise
Mark Victor Hansen The One Minute Millionaire	Owls	Hares	Turtles	Squirrels
Jack Falt Appreciating Differences	Owl	Fox	Beaver	Dolphin
Linda Berens	Owl	Fox	Beaver	Dolphin/Unicorn
Niednagel, 1992	Owl	Humming Bird	Bee	Stork
The Animal System	Bear	Monkey	Beaver	Dolphin
S. Nash – American Plains Indians	Bear	Eagle	Buffalo	Mouse
Spirit Totems Animal Speak	Turkey Vulture	Eagle	Groundhog	Fox
Rosner/Campbell Recession-Time Personalities	Buzzard	Eagle	Ostrich	Chicken-Little
Patty Bogan Managing Your Energy	Shark	Dolphin	Gray Whale	Jellyfish
Sun Bear Medicine Wheel	Thunderbird-Clan	Butterfly-Clan	Turtle-Clan	Frog-Clan

Color "Four Personality Styles" Models

Typical Orientation	Style 1 Results	Style 2 Relationships	Style 3 Tasks	Style 4 Feelings & Emotions
Taylor Hartman – **The Color Code**	**Red-Power**	**Yellow-Fun**	**White-Peace**	**Blue-Intimacy**
The Matrixx System	Gold	Orange	Green	Blue
Don Lowry – **True Colors**	**Gold** Responsible – Be Prepared	**Orange** Spontaneous – Seize the Day	**Green** Conceptual – Knowledge	**Blue** Compassionate – I Care
Career Lifeskills – **Personality Dimensions**	Gold - Organized	Orange - Resourceful	Green - Inquiring	Blue - Authentic
Falt – Appreciating Differences Thru Colors	Gold	Orange	Green	Blue
The Colors People Four Ways System	Gold	Orange	Green	Blue
Real Colors	Gold	Orange	Green	Blue
Tony Alessendra **The Platinum Rule**	**Green**	**Red**	**Yellow**	**Blue**
Dr. Max Luscher – **4 Color Person**	**Red**	Blue	Green	Yellow
Jerry Clark – **The Magic of Colors**	Red	Blue	Green	Yellow
Carol Ritberger – **What Color is Your Personality?**	Red	Orange	Green	Yellow
Color Your World	Red	Orange	Green	Blue
The Birkmann Method	Red	Yellow	Green	Blue
Peak Performance Systems, Inc.	**Red**	Yellow	Green	Blue
Medicine Wheel (several sources)	Blue or Black	Yellow	White	Red

218

Adversarial "Four Personality Styles" Models

Typical Orientation	Style 1 Results	Style 2 Relationships	Style 3 Tasks	Style 4 Feelings & Emotions
James R. Quinn *The Four Fear-Based Reactions*	Fight	Flight	Freeze	Facade
Robin Rinaldi **Four Stress Responses**	Fight	Flight	Freeze	Submission
Rosenban/Seligman **Personality Disorders**	Paranoid	Histrionic	Avoidant	Dependent
Robert E. Lefton **Effective Motivation**	Dominant-Hostile	Dominant-Warm	Submissive-Hostile	Submissive-Warm
James Redfield *The Celestine Prophesy*	Intimidator	Interrogator	Aloof	Poor Me
Virginia Satir	Blamer	Distracter	Computer	Placater
Ernst Kretschmer **Four Temperaments**	Hyperesthetic	Hypomanic	Melancholic	Anesthetic
Pioneer Stereo **Extreme Sports**	Abort	Distort	Delay	Distrust
Jay Hall **Conflict Management**	Win-Lose	Lose-Leave	Yield-Lose	Synergistic
Bartholomew **Attachment Styles**	Dismissing	Insecure	Pre-Occupied	Fearful
James R. Quinn **BlackBerry Abusers**	Controlling	Hurried	Over-Analytical	Worried
Donald T. Simpson **Conflict Styles**	Power	Integration	Denial	Suppression
Personal Strategies	Power	Recognition	Respect	Approval
Cosmopolitan Four Guys You Shouldn't Date	Smooth Operator	Adrenaline Junkie	Work-A-Holic	Nice Guy
Thomas/Kilmann **Conflict Mode**	Competing	Collaborating	Avoiding	Accommodating

Still More "Four Personality Styles" Models

Typical Orientation	Style 1 Results	Style 2 Relationships	Style 3 Tasks	Style 4 Feelings & Emotions
Stephen Covey "The Four Dimensions of Renewal" ... *The 7 Habits of Highly Effective People*	Values & Commitment **Spiritual**	Stress Reduction **Physical**	Reading & Visualizing **Mental**	Service & Empathy **Emotional**
James H. Quinn **LifeStream**	Spiritual	Physical	Mental	Emotional
Alexander Everett Mind Dynamics	**Spiritual**	**Physical**	**Mental**	**Emotional**
Connie Chandler **Paths of Mastery**	Spiritual	Physical	Intellectual	Emotional
Alan David Reed **Holistic Systems**	Ethereal	Material	Conceptual	Emotional
J. Janes **Introcosm** Core/Self	Agency	Physical Unity	Self History	Emotions
Anita Renfroe **Purse-sonalities**	Purse – Tiny Toter	Purse – More is Better	Purse – Monogamous	Purse – Schizophrenic
Florence Littauer **Personality Plus**	Choleric (Powerful)	Sanguine (Popular)	Melancholic (Perfect)	Phlegmatic (Peaceful)
Herb Shephard Philosopher	Perspective	Tone	Autonomy	Connectedness
Cindy Ashton **What Type of Receiver Are You?**	Receiver	Reciprocator	Diminisher	Justifier
James R. Quinn **GET OVER YOURSELF** Keynote Address	"Z"	**Circle**	**Triangle**	**Square**

220

Even More "Four Personality Styles" Models

Typical Orientation	Style 1 Results	Style 2 Relationships	Style 3 Tasks	Style 4 Feelings & Emotions
C. S. Lewis *The Four Loves*	Charity	Eros	Friendship	Affection
Brewer/Ainsworth/Wynne *Power Management*	Active Competitive	Persuasive Interactive	Precise Systematic	Willing Steady
Dranitsaris Sage Personality Profile	Traditionalists	Catalysts	Visionaries	Pragmatists
Actual Me Personality Types	Concluder	Interactor	Analyzer	Synthesizer
Ned Herman *The Whole Brain Business Book*	**Organize**	**Strategize**	**Analyze**	**Personalize**
Warren Berger The Four Phases of Design Thinking	Question	Connect	Commit	Care
Wriths/Bowman-Kruhm *Are You My Type?*	Organizing & Belonging	Acting & Impacting	Understanding & Knowing	Caring & Questioning
Wriths/Bowman-Kruhm *I Need to Get Along With Different Types of People*	Members	Actors	Thinkers	Friends
Allan Pease *Questions are the Answers*	Key #4 Get a Commitment	Key #3 Press the Hot Button	Key #2 Find the Hot Button	Key #1 Melt the Ice
Hersey & Blanchard *Situational Leadership*	Telling	**Selling**	**Delegating**	**Participating**
Caliper Corporation **Profile Personality Assessment Tool**	Problem Solving & Decision Making	Persuasive	Personal Organization & Time Management	Inter-Personal
Sean Covey **7 Habits of Highly Effective Teens**	Bananas	Oranges	Melons	Grapes
James R. Quinn *The Love-Based Leader*	Ethics	**Enthusiasm**	**Evaluation**	**Empathy**

Lets have some fun. What do you think of these?

Typical Orientation	Style 1 Results	Style 2 Relationships	Style 3 Tasks	Style 4 Feelings & Emotions
Disneyland & Disney World	Adventureland	Fantasyland	Tomorrowland	Main Street USA
Biblical Figures	Solomon	David	Abraham	Moses
The Beatles	John Lennon	Paul McCartney	George Harrison	Ringo Starr
The Monkees	Mike Nesmith	Micky Dolenz	Peter Tork	Davy Jones
Countries	Japan China England	USA France Australia	Germany Egypt Switzerland	Russia New Zealand Canada
Leadership Model	Queen Elizabeth	P.T. Barnum	Albert Einstein	Mahatma Gandhi
Roger Hamilton The Billionaires	Martha Stewart	Donald Trump	Sam Walton	Warren Buffett
U.S. Presidents	George Washington Franklin Roosevelt Lyndon Johnson	John Kennedy Ronald Reagan William Clinton	Abraham Lincoln Richard Nixon George H.W. Bush	Gerald Ford Jimmy Carter George W. Bush
2008 Presidential Candidates	Hillary Clinton	Barack Obama	Mitt Romney	John McCain

222

How About These TV Shows?

Typical Orientation	Style 1 Results	Style 2 Relationships	Style 3 Tasks	Style 4 Feelings & Emotions
I Love Lucy	Ricky Ricardo	Lucy Ricardo	Ethel Mertz	Fred Mertz
The Honeymooners	Alice Camden – Audrey Meadows	Ralph Camden – Jackie Gleason	Tricia Norton – Joyce Randolph	Ed Norton – Art Carney
M.A.S.H.	Margaret Houlihan	Hawkeye Pierce	Trapper John	Frank Burns
Magnum P.	Higgins	Thomas Magnum	A.J.	Rick
Little House on the Prairie	Michael Landon	Melissa Gilbert	Melissa Sue Anderson	Karen Grassle
Bonanza	Ben	Little Joe	Adam	Hoss
All In The Family	Archie	Gloria	Michael	Edith
The Beverly Hillbillies	Granny - Daisy Moses	Jethro Bodine	Jed Clampett	Elly May Clampett
Mary Tyler Moore	Mr. Grant	Ted	Murray	Mary
Frasier	Martin Crane	Frasier Crane	Niles Crane	Daphne Moon
Happy Days	The Fonz	Ralph Malph	Potsie	Richie Cunningham
Seinfeld	Elaine	Kramer	Jerry	George
Sex in the City	Miranda	Samantha	Charlotte	Carrie
Desperate Housewives	Lynette	Gabrielle	Bree	Susan

Or These Animations?

Typical Orientation	Style 1 Results	Style 2 Relationships	Style 3 Tasks	Style 4 Feelings & Emotions
The Flintstones	Wilma Flintstone	Fred Flintstone	Betty Rubble	Barney Rubble
The Jetsons	Jane	Judy	Elroy	George
Walt Disney	Donald Duck	Goofy	Scrooge McDuck	Mickey Mouse
Winnie The Pooh	Rabbit	Tigger	Eeyore	Pooh
Peanuts	Lucy	Peppermint Patty	Linus	Charlie Brown
Looney Toons	Daffy Duck	Bugs Bunny	Wiley Coyote	Elmer Fudd
Jim Henson **The Muppets**	Miss Piggy	Kermit The Frog	The Count	Elmo
Alice in Wonderland	Queen of Hearts	Mad Hatter	Caterpillar	Alice
Super Heroes	Wonder Woman	Superman	Batman	Spiderman
The Incredibles	Elastigirl	Dash	Violet	Mr. Incredible
Rocky & Bullwinkle	Boris Badinoff	Rocky	Natasha	Bullwinkle
South Park	Eric Cartman	Kyle Brofloski	Kenny	Stan Marsh
The Simpson's	Bart	Homer	Lisa	Marge

Or These Movies?

Typical Orientation	Style 1 Results	Style 2 Relationships	Style 3 Tasks	Style 4 Feelings & Emotions
Beverly Hills Cop	Lt. Bogomil Ronny Cox	Dt. Axel Foley Eddie Murphy	Dt. Taggart John Ashton	Dt. Rosewood Judge Reinhold
The Dream Team	Jack – Peter Boyle	Billy – Michael Keaton	Henry – Christopher Lloyd	Albert – Stephen Furst
Fantastic Four	Ben Grimm The Thing	Johnny Storm The Human Torch	Reed Richards Mr.Fantastic	Sue Storm/Richards Invisible Girl/Woman
Ferris Bueller's Day Off	Jeanie Bueller Jennifer Grey	Ferris Bueller Matthew Broderick	Cameron Frye Alan Ruck	Sloane Peterson Mia Sara
Ghostbusters	Dana Barrett Sigourney Weaver	Peter Venkman Bill Murray	Egon Spengler Harold Ramis	Ray Stantz Dan Aykroyd
Harry Potter	Hermione Granger Emma Watson	Harry Potter Daniel Radcliffe	Dumbledore – Richard Harris & Michael Gambon	Ron Weasley Rupert Grint
The Lion, the Witch, and the Wardrobe	Peter – William Moeley	Lucy – Georgie Henley	Susan – Anna Popplewell	Edmund – Skandar Keynes
Pirates of the Caribbean	Barbossa – Geoffey Rush	Jack Sparrow Johnny Depp	Will Turner Orlando Bloom	Elizabeth Swann Keira Knightley
Rocky	Rocky Balboa Sylvester Stallone	Apollo Creed Carl Weathers	Mickey Goldmill Burgess Meredith	Adrian Pennino Talia Shire
Silverado	Emmett – Scott Glenn	Jake – Kevin Costner	Mal Jonson – Danny Glover	Paden – Kevin Kline
Stand By Me	Chris – River Phoenix	Teddy – Corey Feldman	Gordie – Wil Wheaton	Vern – Jery O'Connell
Star Wars	Princess Leia Carrie Fisher	Han Solo Harrison Ford	Obi-Wan Kenobi Alec Guinness	Luke Skywalker Mark Hamill
Top Gun	Charlie – Kelly McGillis	Maverick – Tom Cruise	Iceman – Val Kilmer	Goose – Anthony Edwards
The Wizard of Oz	Scarecrow – Ray Bolger	Cowardly Lion – Bert Lahr	Dorothy – Judy Garland	Tin Man – Jack Haley

And For All You "Trekkers" *

Typical Orientation	Style 1 Results	Style 2 Relationships	Style 3 Tasks	Style 4 Feelings & Emotions
Star Trek	James T. Kirk	Scotty	Spock	Dr. Leonard McCoy
The Next Generation	Jean-Luc Picard	William T. Riker	Data	Deanna Troi
Deep Space Nine	Benjamin Sisko	Quark	Odo	Dr. Julian Bashir
Voyager	Kathryn Janeway	Neelix	Tuvok	B'Elanna Torres
Enterprise	Jonathan Archer	Charles Tucker	T'Pol	Dr. Phlox

* The correct term for zealous Star Trek fans is "Trekkers" and not "Trekkies," according to Leonard Nimoy (Mr. Spock of Star Trek).

WORLDWIDE PRAISE

"The Love-Based Leader is an extraordinary manual for creating results by overcoming negativity and fear-based reactions. I have found the concepts and techniques to be effective across cultural boundaries and personal backgrounds. It will change how organizations conduct their affairs."
John Nemanic – Ontario, CANADA
Chairman/Founder: GeeksForLess.com, Hostopia.com, and Tucows.com

"There are few short cuts to a truly rewarding life. Nevertheless, The Love-Based Leader offers a leg up to those seeking more successful personal and professional relationships."
Robert H. Sanders – Illinois, USA
Public Relations – Chicago Tribune, WTTW, Playboy, TV Guide

"The Love-Based Leader has enhanced our salespeople's understanding of our client's needs and motivations, particularly in stressful situations. I can directly attribute many of our successes to Quinn's tools and strategies."
Michael Pinkney – NEW ZEALAND
Director, ReMax North Shore

"Since I started using the tools from The Love-Based Leader, my employees, partners, and customers regularly ask me what's the secret of my effectiveness and productivity. The answer: I base my leadership style on the principles in this book every day, both at work and at home."
Fred Dewey - California & New York, USA
CEO, Kachingle.com

"The Love-Based Leader is brilliant. I'd fallen into a rut. You have given me the tools to break out of old patterns. My hat's off to you."
Rena Gaile – Ontario, CANADA
1997 runner-up to Shania Twain for, "Canadian Female Artist of the Year"

"I've noticed immediate effects with the way our managers are relating to others. They've gained the ability to step back from negative reactions and refocus on their initial objectives. The Love-Based Leader workshop is impressive."
Michael Mahanger – New York, USA
Director, Microtel Corporation

"The Love-Based Leader gets people to look at themselves in an honest and non-judgmental way. Instead of justifying or denying ineffective behaviors, readers will gain the ability to create desired results in their lives."
Jim Morgan – Ontario, CANADA
Emmy Award Winning TV Theme Producer & Writer
Care Bears, Beetlejuice, and The Adventures of Tin Tin

227

"*The Love-Based Leader* has helped me to heal and expand my personal relationships. With it, I have also become a more effective lobbyist, director, parent, and restaurant manager. It is a key to creating life successes."
Nan Hanna-Paquin – New York, USA
Professional Lobbyist, Partner H/P Associates

"The beauty of *The Love-Based Leader* is that this powerful book can be picked up and read at any point, as a constant reference source."
Dustin Hotrum – Ontario, CANADA
CEO, H.M.T Sales Tax Consultants Inc.

"This book is a primer of the basics for happiness. The concepts in *The Love-Based Leader* are presented simply, with humor and from the heart. A winning combination."
Phyllis Campagna – Illinois, USA
Business Coach, XSEL Performance Strategies

PART ONE: "I started reading *The Love-Based Leader*, but made the mistake of telling my husband, Morgan, about your wonderful book. I haven't seen it since. I can't wait to get it back."
Joanne Cotten – Illinois, USA

PART TWO: "I have been devouring *The Love-Based Leader*. Having read Carnegie's "How to Win Friends & Influence People", Waitley's "The Psychology of Winning", Burg's "Winning Without Intimidation", Covey's "The 7 Habits of Highly Effective People", and Littauer's "Personality Plus", I've found this book better at putting it all together in one source. It's great."
Morgan Cotten – Illinois, USA
Deputy Director of Transportation for DuPage County

"*The Love-Based Leader* is an incredible tool for business and personal life. This book has more immediately applicable lessons and techniques than all the leadership books I have read put together. This is a great book."
J. André Kennedy – Ontario, CANADA
President, Golf To The Nth Degree Inc.

"*The Love-Based Leader* provides immediate insight building relationships in the family and workplace. You will learn ideas you can put into practice the very day you begin reading this practical and delightful book."
Cindy Clark Hoy – California, USA
Teacher (Redondo Union High School), Certificated Alcohol & Drug Counselor

"*The Love-Based Leader* is a powerfully insightful and often humorous roadmap of how to control myself when I want different outcomes."
Ross Stokes – NEW ZEALAND
CEO, IP Marketing Group Ltd.

228

"Thank you for illuminating human behavior in a way that is fun to read and simple to follow. It just plain makes sense. *The Love-Based Leader* gives readers the tools to change their reactive patterns to become happier and more successful. I am personally indebted to you for making my journey easier."
Dr. Ross S. Royster – Wisconsin, USA
34 years as a practicing Chiropractor

"My initial perusal turned into a must-read-sit-down. *The Love-Based Leader* goes to the heart and soul of successful communications. I am recommending this amazing book to fellow lawyers and my hospital clients."
Gail Allyn Landau, Esq. – California, USA
Medical Malpractice Defense Attorney and Risk Management Consultant

"*The Love-Based Leader* provides practical and useful information in a clear format, permitting tangible and immediate benefits. The combination of concise text and evocative imagery is very effective."
David Bryan – Ontario, CANADA
Registered Trade Mark Agent and Partner, Gowling Lafleur Henderson LLP

"*The Love-Based Leader* has enhanced our salespeople's understanding of our client's needs and motivations, particularly in stressful situations. I can directly attribute many of our successes to Quinn's tools and strategies."
Chef Dana Gumataotao – Hawaii, USA
President, Okey Dokey Productions, Inc.
Host, *The Sugar Cane Shack* – Hawaii's new and exciting cooking show!

"I have read over one hundred self-help books and have found the most valuable lessons for success in *The Love-Based Leader.* This is a great book."
Philip Barry Greig – Auckland, NEW ZEALAND

"*The Love-Based Leader* is fabulous! James Roswell Quinn has great insight into what is needed so badly in today's society."
Elizabeth Bennett, M.Ed – California, USA
Author, *Peer Abuse Know More: Bullying From a Psychological Perspective*

"*The Love-Based Leader* has the power to change lives for the better. This is a valuable book."
Jillian Jeffery – Ontario, CANADA
Associate Editor, RENOVATION & DÉCOR Magazine

"*The Love-Based Leader* allows the reader to see how they can respond to negativity in a way that all parties benefit. Quinn's models and examples guide the reader to an understanding of how love-based choices can make our lives work so much better."
Steve Aman -- New York, USA
President, Sanctuary at Crowfield Farm

"The Love-Based Leader is a wonderful tool for my personal and professional growth. Every corporation and household should own a copy of this masterpiece."
Nancy May – Illinois, USA
Teacher, "Yoga from the Heart"

"The Love-Based Leader is without question, one of the most remarkable and captivating books I have ever read. It should be required reading."
Emily Cieslinski – Ontario, CANADA
MLM & Direct Distribution Marketing Expert

"The Love-Based Leader is packed with advice on how to deal with others by managing your own reactions. More importantly, the advice works. The way this book is organized makes it easy to use as a reference."
Rudy Bazelmans – New Hampshire, USA
Director of Professional Services, Phonetic Systems

"This important work is practical and enduring. *The Love-Based Leader* is relevant to my life. The exercises helped me to put the lessons into practice."
Chris J. Cuciurean – Ontario, CANADA
Business Coach and President, LifeLeaders

"I have had immediate results from *The Love-Based Leader*. Simple things, like getting my teenage son to make his bed, certainly please me. However, that I have stopped my old and tiresome complaining routine has made me even happier. This is an outstanding result for me. Awesome!"
Geoff Woods – AUSTRALIA

"The bottom line of *The Love-Based Leader* is that the principles in work. It is amazing the influence you can have when you are in control of yourself."
Tom Dusmet – Ontario, CANADA
Investment Advisor with a Major Bank Owned Brokerage Firm

"During the last 20 years I have spent thousands of dollars on Self-Help, Self-Improvement, and Motivational Lectures, CD's, Tapes, Videos, and Seminars. I have made in-depth studies of Quantum Physics, the Law of Attraction, and Religion. However it was not until I read *The Love Based Leader* that it all came together. I learned more from your words than all of it. I will never be able to thank you enough. I needed the healing."
Patricia Gaines – California, USA
Multi Level Marketing Expert

"The Love-Based Leader inspires me to never stay stuck, and to continue on to my next opportunity/experience in life.
Debbie Bohunicky – Ontario, CANADA
Personal Development Coach/Bereavement Facilitator, Niagara Workshops

"I have worked with Quinn since 1978. After all these years, it's a privilege to see him sharing himself with the world. James Roswell Quinn is a gifted teacher."

Alexander Everett – Oregon, USA

"Father of the Human Potential Movement"

Founder, Pendragon School at Bexhill-on-Sea, Sussex, England, 1950
Founder, Shiplake College at Henley-on-Thames, Oxford, England, 1953
Founder, Fort Worth Country Day School, 1963
Creator and teacher, Mind Dynamics (self-improvement seminar), 1968
Subject of the book, *The Power of Alpha Thinking*, Jess Stearn, 1969
Creator and teacher, Inward Bound (spiritual seminar), 1973
Creator and teacher, Love, Life & Light (spiritual retreat & seminar), 1988
Subject of the book, *Inward Bound*, Billie Sargent Hatchell, 1991
Author, *The Genius Within You* (audio program), Nightingale-Conant, 1991
Author, *Inner Wealth*, (audio program), Nightingale-Conant, 1992
Author, *Inward Bound – Living Life From The Inside Out*, 1998
Author, *Cosmic Consciousness* (CD ROM AudioBook), 2001

"The Teacher of Teachers"

Russell Bishop (Insight Seminars)
Stuart Emery (Actualizations)
Werner Erhardt ("est" and Landmark Forum)
John Hanley (Lifespring)
Howard Nease (Personal Dynamics)
James & Janet Quinn (LifeStream)
Dr. O. Carl Simonton (The Simonton Cancer Center)
Randy Revell (Context Trainings)
Robert White (Life Dynamics and ARC)
Tom & Jane Willhite (PSI World)

BIBLIOGRAPHY

Alessandra, Tony & Cathcart, Jim, *Relationship Strategies*, Nightingale-Conant

Ansari, Mahfooz, *Managing People at Work: Leadership Styles and Influence Strategies*, Sage Publications, 1991

Arrien, Angeles, *The Four Fold Way*, Harper San Francisco, 1993

Atkins, Stuart, *The Name of Your Game: Four Game Plans for Success*, Ellis & Stewart, 1982

Bamborough, J.B.; Dodsworth, Martin; & Burton, *Robert; Anatomy of Melancholy* (Vol 6), Clarendon Press, 2001

Baron, Renee, *What Type Am I: Discover Who You Really Are*, Penguin, 1998

Bartholomew, *Avoidance of Intimacy: An Attachment Perspective.* Journal of Social & Personal Relationships, 1990

Batra, Dr. Ravi, *The Great Depression of 1990*, Simon and Schuster, 1987

Berens, Linda V., *Understanding Yourself and Others, An Introduction to Temperament*, Telos Publications, 2000

Benson, Herbert, *The Relaxation Response*, HarperCollins Publishers, 2000

Bolton, Robert & Dorothy, G., *Social Style/Management Style*, AMACOM, 1984

Brewer, Ainsworth, & Wynne, *G. E., Power Management*, Prentice-Hall, 1984

Bristol, Claude, *The Magic of Believing*, Pocket Books, 1994

Buscalia, Leo, *Love*, Ballantine Books, 1996

Clark, Jerry, *The Magic of Colors*, Club Rhino, Inc.

Combs, Jeffrey, *The Animal Factor*, Golden Mastermind Seminars, Inc.

Covey, Stephen, *7 Habits of Highly Effective People*, Simon & Schuster 1990

Davidson, Jacqueline, *Develop Your Best Self*, Toastmaster Magazine, May 2004

De Ville, Jard, *Nice Guys Finish First*, William Morrow, 1979

Dryden, Gordon & Vos, Jeannette, *The Learning Revolution*, Jalmar Press, 1994

Everett, Alexander, *Inward Bound, Living Life From The Inside Out*, Bookpartners Inc, 1998

Fuller, R. Buckminster, *Critical Path*, St. Martin's Press, 2002

Ganza, Ann, *Journey of Hope, Remembering Mother Teresa's Spirit*, Agnel Publishing, 2001

Gray, Dr John, *Men Are From Mars Women Are From Venus*, Harper Collins, 1993

Geier, John G., *(D.I.S.C.) Personal Profile System*, Performax Systems International, 1977

Hansen, Mark Victor, *The One Minute Millionaire*, Harmony Books, 2002

Harris, Thomas A., MD, *I'm OK – You're OK*, Galahad, 2004 (revised)

Hartman, Taylor, PhD, *The Color Code*, Scribner, 1987

Hawkins, David R., *Power vs. Force*, Hay House, 2002

Herrmann, Ned, *The Creative Brain*, Brain Books, 1991

Herrmann, Ned, *The Whole Brain Business Book*, McGraw-Hill, 1996

Hill, Napoleon, *Think and Grow Rich*, Fawcett Books, 1990

Hill, Richard, *The Best of Organization Development*, American Society for Training Development, 1988

Horrell, Edward, *More Than Words*, e-book

Hunsaker, Phillip L., *The Art of Managing People*, Prentice Hall, 1980

Hurley, Joanna, *Mother Teresa*, Courage Books, 1997

Jampolski, Jerry, *Love is Letting Go of Fear*, Celestial Arts, 1988

Jaynes, J., *The Origin of Consciousness in the Breakdown of the Bicameral Mind*, Houghton Mifflin, 1977

Johnson, Spencer, M.D., *Who Moved My Cheese?*, J.P. Putnam's Sons, 1998

Jung, Carl Gustav, *Psychological Types (Collected Works of C.G. Jung Vol.6)*, Princeton University Press, 1976

Keirsey, David, *Please Understand Me. Character & Temperament Types*, Prometheus, 1984

Lefton, Robert E., *Effective Motivation Through Performance Appraisal*, Wiley & Sons, 1977

LeTellier, John, *Quantum Learning*, Dell Publishing, 1992

Lewis, C.S., *The Four Loves*, Harvest Books, 1971

Ley, D. Forbes, *The Best Seller*, Sales Success Press, 1984

Littauer, Florence, *PERSONALITY PLUS*, Revell Publishers, 1992

Lovas, Michael, *Face Values*

Luft, Joseph, *Of Human Interaction*, Palo Alto, CA. National Press, 1969

Luscher, Dr. Max, *The 4 Color Person*, Simon & Schuster, 1979

Maltz, Maxwell, *Psychocybernetics*, Pocket Books, 1989

Marston, William M., *Emotions of Normal People*, Personna Press, 1979

Maslow, Abraham, *The Farther Reaches of Human Nature*, Viking Press, 1971

Merrill, David, & Reid, Roger, *Personal Styles & Effective Performance*, Saint Lucie, 1981

Miscisin, Mary, *Showing Our True Colors*, True Colors, Inc, 2001

Montgomery, Richard, *People Patterns: A Modern Guide to the Four Temperaments*

Moore, Robert & Gillette, Douglas, *Rediscovering the Archetypes of the Mature Masculine*, HarperCollins, 1990

Myers, Peter B. & Isabel Briggs, *Gifts Differing: Understanding Personality, Consulting* Psychologists Press, 1997

New International Version, *Holy Bible*, International Bible Society, 1984

Pease, Allan, *Questions are the Answers*, Pease Training International Ltd., 2000

Redfield, James, *The Celestine Prophecy*, Warner Books, 1993

Rowling, JK, *Harry Potter and the Sorcerer's Stone,* Arthur Levine Books, 1997

Ruiz, Don Miguel, *The Four Agreements*, Amber-Publishing, 1997

Saltzman, David, *The Jester Has Lost His Jingle*, Jester Co. Inc., 1995

Seligman, Walker, & Rosenhan, *Abnormal Psychology, 4th Edition*, W.W. Norton & Co, 2000

Sieden, Steven, *Buckminster Fuller's Universe: His Life and Times*, Perseus, 2000

Sperry, Len, *Effective Leadership*, Psychology Press, 2002

Sun Bear, *Medicine Wheel, Earth Astrology*, Fireside, 1980

Stearn, Jess, *The Power of Alpha Thinking*, New American Library, 1989

Teresa, Mother, *A Simple Path*, Ballantine Books, 1995

Wilson Learning Corporation, *Social Styles Sales Strategies*, 1977

A Request For Stories of Love-Based Leadership

We are collecting stories of *Love-Based Leadership* for a future publication. Whether you have created a love-based solution to a negative circumstance or witnessed one, please send us the details. These stories can be personal, relationship, family, professional, community, national, or global in nature.

Please send your stories to:

Quinn Incorporated
The Love-Based Leader
P.O. Box 766
Durand, IL 61024-0766
U.S.A.

Or email your stories to:

Stories@LoveBasedLeader.com

By submitting your stories of *Love-Based Leadership*, you will help others to grow as Love-Based Leaders. Stories, once submitted, become the property of *Quinn Incorporated* and cannot be returned. If multiple entries are received for the same event, the entry with earliest postmark will be used.

234

Contact The Author

[ ] YES   I would like *James Roswell Quinn* to contact me.
I understand that I am under no obligation, and all information
that I share is confidential.

I am primarily interested in:

[ ] Corporate Consulting   [ ] Financial Literacy Workshop
[ ] Keynote Address   [ ] Success Coaching
[ ] Leadership Retreat   [ ] Sales/Management Workshop
[ ] Bulk Purchases of Books & CDs [ ] Becoming a Booking Agent

[ ] Other _____

My key frustrations or needs are:

[ ] Personal Health   [ ] Personal Relationships
[ ] Personal Finance   [ ] Self-Worth and/or Self-Esteem
[ ] Business Health   [ ] Business Relationships
[ ] Creating Teamwork   [ ] Reducing Employee Turnover
[ ] Developing a Organizational Culture of Problem-Solving by Consensus
[ ] Other _____

My Name: _____

Business Name: _____

Address: _____

City: _____

State: _____ Country _____ Postal/Zip _____

Phone: _____ email: _____

Type of Business/Products/Services: _____

Years in Business: _____ # Employees: _____

# of Locations: _____ # Owners/Partners: _____

eMail this completed page to: **Quinn@LoveBasedLeader.com**

... or Mail to:

Quinn Incorporated, **P.O. Box 766, Durand, IL 61024-0766**

GET OVER YOURSELF
8-CD Personal Audio Seminar

- Change Can Be Fun -

If you have ever considered yourself to be your own worst enemy, and are ready to get out of your own way, then you will LOVE this acclaimed 8-CD Personal Audio Seminar.

Take advantage of Quinn's unparalleled experience of three decades of facilitating over 1,500 personal growth seminars, and coaching dozens of millionaires, worldwide.

GET OVER YOURSELF
ONLY $199.95 USD

You have nothing to lose, and **everything** to gain, as these CDs come with a 90-Day Unconditional Guarantee!

This is an AMAZING VALUE.
You would have to attend all 4 of Quinn's seminars, and his keynote address, to get all of these tools and concepts!

(Total VALUE: $2,999.95)

To order your copy, go to "**The Quinn Store**" link at:

http://www.TheLoveBasedLeader.com

... and check out Quinn's outrageous:

GET OVER YOURSELF STORE
http://www.CafePress.com/QuinnStore

6895136R1

Made in the USA
Charleston, SC
21 December 2010